AMERICAN VOICES FROM

The Great Depression

AMERICAN VOICES FROM

The Great Depression

Adriane Ruggiero

Withdrawn

BENCHMARK BOOKS

MARSHALL CAVENDISH
NEW YORK

FOR M, WHO LIVED IT

Benchmark Books
Marshall Cavendish
99 White Plains Road
Tarrytown, New York 10591-9001
www.marshallcavendish.com

Copyright © 2005 by Marshall Cavendish Corporation

Library of Congress Cataloging-in-Publication Data
Ruggiero, Adriane.
The Great Depression / by Adriane Ruggiero.
p. cm. — (American voices from—)
Includes bibliographical references and index.
ISBN 0-7614-1696-X
1. United States—History—1933–1945—Sources—Juvenile literature.
2. Depressions—1929—United States—Sources—Juvenile literature. 3. United States—History—1919–1933—Sources—Juvenile literature. 4. United States—Economic conditions—1918–1945—Sources—Juvenile literature. I. Title. II. Series.

E806.R865 2004   973.917—dc22
2004000865

Printed in China
1 3 5 6 4 2

Series design and composition by Anne Scatto / PIXEL PRESS
Photo Research by Linda Sykes Picture Research, Inc., Hilton Head, S.C.

The photographs in this book are used by permission and through the courtesy of:
The Granger Collection: cover, ii, xii, xiii, xix, 2, 4, 41, 48, 59, 67, 78, 83, 92, 107 (top), 108 (bottom); FDR Library, Hyde Park, NY/The New Yorker ©Conde Nast: viii; Brown Brothers: xi, hx, xxii, 7, 11 20, 25, 29, 33, 36, 39, 44, 68, 71, 72, 77, 90, 94; Corbis: xiv, 102, 106 (bottom), 106 (top), 108 (top), 109; Horace Bristol/Corbis: xvi; Museum of American Political History, University of Hartford: 17; Bettmann/Corbis: 22, 61, 63, 99; Minnesota Historical Society/Corbis: 53; Whitney Museum of American Art, New York; Purchase 36.148: 56; Library of Congress: 81, 97; Russell Baker, Growing Up, Congden and Weed, Inc., New York. 1982: 84

ON THE COVER: Effects of the stock market crash: a desperate man must sell his car.

ON THE TITLE PAGE: A 1938 cartoon, entitled *One Person out of Every Ten*, depicts the plight of many Americans who had to stand in line for soup and bread in order to survive.

Acknowledgments

Permission has been granted to use quotations from the following copyrighted works:

"Berry Picker" by John Macnamara. Reprinted with permission from the September 12, 1934, issue of *The Nation.*

"Brother, Can You Spare a Dime?" by E. Y. "Yip" Harburg & Jay Gorney. © 1932, renewed Glocca Morra Music & Gorney Music. Administered by Next Decade Entertainment, Inc. All rights reserved. Used by permission.

"A Call to Action" by Robert LaFollette. Reprinted with permission from the July 15, 1931, issue of *The Nation.*

"A Choice of Weapons" by Gordon Parks. Copyright © 1965, 1966 by Gordon Parks. © renewed 1994 by Gordon Parks. Reprinted by permission of HarperCollins Publishers Inc.

Down and Out in the Great Depression: Letters from the Forgotten Man by Robert S. McElvaine. © 1983 by the University of North Carolina Press. Used by permission of the publisher.

"Dust Bowl Refugee." Words and music by Woody Guthrie. © 1960 (renewed) and 1963 (renewed) Ludlow Music, Inc. New York, NY. Used by permission.

First-Person America by Ann Banks. New York: Alfred A. Knopf, 1980. Used by permission of Ann Banks.

Growing Up by Russell Baker. Reprinted by permission of Don Congdon Associates, Inc. © 1982 by Russell Baker.

Hard Times: An Oral History of the Great Depression by Studs Terkel © 1995. Reprinted by permission of The New Press.

"John Doe Gets His Job Through the Indiana State Employment Service" by Robert D. Adams. Reprinted with permission from the October 3, 1937, issue of the *Fort Wayne Journal-Gazette.*

The Secret Diary of Harold L. Ickes, Volume I: The First Thousand Days, 1933–1936 by Harold L. Ickes. © 1953 by Simon & Schuster, Inc. © renewed 1981 by Harold M. Ickes and Elizabeth Ickes. Reprinted with permission of Simon & Schuster Adult Publishing Group.

"Why Ford Workers Strike" by Carl M. Mydans. Reprinted with permission from the October 25, 1933, issue of *The Nation.*

Contents

Mar. 4, 1933   THE   Price 15 cents

NEW YORKER

Peter Arno

Old newspapers and magazines are a great source of wealth to historians studying primary sources. This amusing *New Yorker* magazine cover depicts a smiling Franklin D. Roosevelt *(right)* on his inauguration day traveling next to a frowning Herbert Hoover, the outgoing president. The wit and good humor of the illustration never saw the light of day, however: because of an attempt on Roosevelt's life, the Inauguration Day cover never appeared on newsstands.

About Primary Sources

What Is a Primary Source?

In the pages that follow, you will be hearing many different "voices" from a special time in America's past. Some of the selections are long and others are short. You'll find many easy to understand at first reading, while others may require several readings. All the selections have one thing in common, however. They are primary sources. This is the name historians give to the bits and pieces of information that make up the record of human existence. Primary sources are important to us because they are the very essence, the core material for all historical investigation. You might call them "history" itself.

Primary sources *are* evidence; they give historians the all-important clues they need to understand the past. Perhaps you have read a detective story in which a sleuth must solve a mystery by piecing together bits of evidence he or she uncovers. The detective makes deductions, or educated guesses based on the evidence, and solves the mystery once all the deductions point in a certain direction. Historians work in much the same way. Like detectives, historians analyze data through careful reading and rereading. After much analysis, they draw conclusions about an event, a person, or an entire era. Different historians may analyze the same evidence and come to different conclusions. That is why there is often sharp disagreement about an event.

Primary sources are also called *documents*—a rather dry word to describe what can be just about anything: an official speech by a government leader, an old map, an act of Congress, a letter worn out from too much handling, an entry hastily scrawled into a diary, a detailed newspaper account of an event, a funny or sad song, a colorful poster, a cartoon, a faded photograph, or someone's remembrance captured on tape or film.

By examining the following documents, you, the reader, will be taking on the role of historian. Here is your chance to immerse yourself in a specific time—the Great Depression. You'll come to know the voices of the men and women who lived during those years when Americans experienced poverty, hunger, and hopelessness. You'll read the letters they wrote to their president, the diary entries they penned, the songs they wrote—the words they used to express their thoughts about what was happening around them.

How to Read a Primary Source

Each document in this book deals with the Great Depression and America's reaction to that turbulent time in its history. Some of the documents are from government publications. Others are from the official papers of President Franklin D. Roosevelt and the men and women in his administration. Many of the documents are letters written by ordinary people asking for help—to buy food, to pay debts, to survive. All of the documents, major and minor, help us to understand what it was like to live during the Great Depression.

As you read each document, ask yourself some basic questions. Who is writing? What is the writer's point of view? Who is the writer's audience? What is he or she trying to tell that audience? Is the message clearly expressed or is it implied, that is, stated indirectly?

Tuesday, October 29, 1929— the day the stock market crashed—made alarming headlines in *The New York Times*.

DEMOCRACY

Cartoons are a great window on the past. They are an effective way to get a message across, too. The cartoon above has a one-word caption: "Democracy." What point do you think the cartoonist is making? After you finish reading this book, turn back to this page and see what other thoughts the cartoon may inspire.

What words does the writer use to convey his or her message? Are the words emotion-filled or objective in tone? If you are looking at a photograph, examine it carefully, taking in all the details. Where do you think it was taken? What is happening in the foreground? In the background? Is it posed or is it an action shot? How can you tell? Who do you think took the picture, and what is its purpose?

These are questions that help you think critically about a primary source.

Some tools have been included with the documents to help you in your investigations. Unusual words have been defined near where they appear. Thought-provoking questions follow many of the documents. They help focus your reading so that you can get the most out of the document. As you read each selection, you'll probably come up with many questions of your own. That's great! The work of a historian always leads to many, many questions. Some can be answered, while others require more investigation. Perhaps when you finish this book, your questions will lead you to further explorations of one of the most trying periods in American history—the Great Depression.

When Franklin Roosevelt took office in 1933 and promised Americans a "new deal" to bring the country out of the Depression, a cartoonist took the opportunity to comment. Here Roosevelt is leading Congress in a mad dash to pass new laws.

A migrant farmworker and his child, outside their makeshift
home in California's Imperial Valley, 1937. The devastating effects of
the Great Depression thrust people all over the country into poverty.

Introduction

CRISIS STRIKES AMERICA

The Great Depression of the 1930s was the worst economic crisis in American history. It brought the economy of the United States to a near standstill, caused hardship and suffering for millions, and affected nations throughout the world. What made the Depression's impact so powerful was the fact that it followed a period of relative prosperity and optimism. That era came to an abrupt end when the stock market crashed in 1929. Historians now agree that the Crash itself did not cause the Depression. Its psychological effect was huge, however. Americans looked to the nation's banking and business leaders for answers to what caused the financial crisis, but none came. They looked to President Herbert Hoover for help when businesses closed their doors and workers were laid off. His promise that "prosperity is just around the corner" rang false when the economy failed to recover. The Depression reached its depths in 1933 when approximately one-fourth of Americans—some 15 million people—were jobless, and it did not begin to ease until 1939 when World War II broke out in Europe. With that tumultuous event, American industries and

Child labor increased during the Great Depression as families struggled to survive. Hours spent laboring in factories, fields, and even mines kept many younger children out of school. In some families, parents sent older children away from home in search of work.

workers began to harness themselves to the job of producing planes, ships, and weapons for the nation's allies. America's participation in the war, beginning in 1941, helped lift the country out of the Depression as all attention shifted to the task of fighting and winning a global war.

Historians and economists continue to debate the causes of the Great Depression. They point to easy credit and buying on credit, the unequal distribution of wealth between American workers and corporate executives, an excess of profits in the hands of industry, overproduction of farm produce and consumer goods, underconsumption of these products by the public, the weakness of labor unions, and overspeculation in the stock market, to name a few factors. All of these were elements of the business environment during the years following the end of World War I.

Economists and political leaders expect economies to go through periods of growth, slowdowns, and recovery, but the Depression of the 1930s was more severe and lasted longer than any other in U.S. history. During the Depression, there was a dramatic shift in people's perception of the strength of the nation's economy. Their lack of confidence contributed to a prolonged crisis in which prices fell, industrial production slowed down, individuals and businesses went bankrupt, and workers lost their jobs. The economy did not right itself after a few years as business and government leaders had hoped. Instead, it continued its downward spiral. The effects of the decline touched nearly all segments of society and forced Americans to question their economic and political system as never before.

The story of the Great Depression cannot be separated from the presidency of Franklin Delano Roosevelt—often called simply by his initials, FDR—who defeated beleaguered President Hoover in the election of 1932. FDR would go on to lead the United States for an unprecedented twelve years and to craft the New Deal, the name given to his plan to pull America out of the Depression. The plight of jobless Americans began to ease during FDR's first administration (1933–1937), when a wide variety of emergency government programs to relieve human suffering and spur recovery came into existence. Among these programs were the Civilian Conservation Corps (CCC), the National Recovery Administration (NRA), the Agricultural Adjustment Act (AAA), and the Public Works Administration (PWA). There were many others, each known by its own set of initials, amusingly referred to as "alphabet soup." Programs of relief and recovery continued during Roosevelt's second term in office (1937–1941).

Many Americans applauded the New Deal legislation and looked upon Roosevelt as the man who saved them and the nation from ruin. Others were less positive. Some thought Roosevelt's spending on huge public projects was reckless, and they feared placing so much power into the hands of the president. Others felt that Roosevelt and the New Deal did not go far enough in correcting the ills of American society. Hardly anyone who grew up during the Depression was a neutral observer of the events taking place. For too many Americans it was a time of fear, poverty, and insecurity. For others, especially those involved in government, it was an exciting time when new ideas and approaches to solving problems were put into action.

The Depression of the 1930s saw major changes in the relationship between the government and the American people. During the New Deal, the federal government took an active role in the nation's economy; it developed hydroelectric power projects in rural areas, established guidelines and codes for businesses, created jobs, and trained workers. This did not happen without controversy, however. Many people opposed the intrusion of government into the way business was conducted and resented its attempt to

Alphabet soup: a cartoon makes light of FDR's many New Deal programs, which were often referred to by their abbreviated forms.

President Roosevelt *(left)* took office during one of the most trying times in the nation's history. To face the challenge, he put revolutionary ideas to work in an effort to lift the country out of the Depression.

control the economy. They called this "big government." Most Americans, however, were grateful for the government's efforts to provide security and help for the old, the poor, and the disabled. The creation of a national system of social security is one of the most outstanding results of the New Deal legislation. So too are the vast improvements made during the Roosevelt administration to the nation's infrastructure: many of the bridges, highways, national parks, schools, libraries, post offices, and courthouses Americans enjoy today were built during the New Deal.

The Great Depression was one of the most difficult periods in American history. Poverty, hunger, and fear stalked the land. Democracy, the nation's most treasured possession, was at risk. Listening to the voices of the people who lived through the era, we may hear our own parents, grandparents, and great-grandparents speaking. Their voices tell of shock and despair, but also of hope and courage.

New York City's Wall Street on "Black Tuesday," October 29, 1929.
The day marked the beginning of the collapse of the U.S. stock market, an event
that would send shock waves across the nation and the world.

Chapter I

The Shock

O N SEPTEMBER 3, 1929, the prices of shares traded on the nation's stock exchanges reached record-setting levels. Shares of stock in such established companies as General Electric, American Telephone and Telegraph, and U.S. Steel soared to new heights: $396 per share, $304, and $262, respectively. At day's end nearly 45 million shares had been traded. Then, slowly at first, the bubble began to lose air. Later in September, prices began to drop. Most investors were unconcerned, however, and continued to hold their stocks. The market recovered as investors believed it would. They looked forward to greater profits and buying even more shares. And it was so easy to get rich . . . on paper, that is. Then in October the decline began again. On October 23 investors frantically began to sell off their stocks. Much of the value gained in previous months was lost in the morning's trading, and panic selling followed. Stockbrokers were flooded with calls from their clients to SELL! SELL! SELL!

On Thursday, October 24, investors began a feverish sell-off again. By midday, losses had reached about $9 billion. Despite statements of confidence issued by the nation's leading bankers, the market could not be steadied. On Tuesday, October 29 (later called Black Tuesday), the bottom continued to fall out. Stockbrokers gave up all hope of recovering the previous days' losses. The downward movement of the stock market continued through the middle of November, when about $26 billion in investments had been lost. It was the biggest market collapse in U.S. history.

The Crash marked the end of the "Roaring Twenties," a free-wheeling time of invention, social change, and economic expansion that had begun in the years following World War I. Many Americans had achieved a comfortable life in the 1920s. They owned their homes and cars. They went on vacations and bought on credit.

Although most Americans did not own stock in 1929, there were many business opportunities for an eager investor. Trusts and holding companies existed for the sole

A headline in *Variety*, a newspaper for the entertainment industry, jokes about the events of October 29, 1929. But the nation would soon learn that the Crash was nothing to laugh about.

purpose of investing in stocks. Consumers were able to buy shares of stock on margin, that is, by putting a little money down and owing the rest to the broker. Brokers got the money to fund the loans from the nation's banks or major corporations. There were few controls over the stock market. Investors believed that stock prices would go higher and they would get richer. Such hopes were dashed in 1929, and as the gloom spread Americans looked to their president for a solution. In this chapter you will read about how some Americans reacted to the stock market collapse and the Depression that followed.

The End of a "Mad Dream," a Stockbroker Remembers

Many people had placed their life savings in the stock market, and they lost everything in the Crash. John Hersch was a Chicago stockbroker and investor in 1929. Part of his job included keeping the figures on individuals who were carrying stocks on margin. Here is his description of what happened to him on those fateful days in October.

I HAD ABOUT $3,000 in the stock market, which was all the money I had. On Black Friday . . . that margin account went out of the window. I may have had about $62 left. My wife had a . . . $125 a week job with a Shakespearean theater company. That night, she came home . . . and said, "Guess what happened today?" I said, "What?" She said, "I quit." I was making about $60 a week and she was making $125. Two-thirds of our income and all of our savings disappeared in that day.

When the break started, you had a deluge of selling, from weakened margin accounts. We had to stay up all night figuring. . . . Everybody was in trouble.

The guy I worked for was sitting in the wire room, watching the tape. The tape was something to see, because Radio Corporation [a stock] . . . would be ninety-five on the tape . . . they'd flash you sixty on the [trading] floor [of the stock exchange]. The floor was a madhouse.

The Crash hurt not only wealthy business-people, but also ordinary Americans who had invested their savings in the stock market.

The Crash—it didn't happen in one day. There were a great many warnings. The country was crazy. . . . It was a mad dream of get-rich-quick.

You had no governmental control of margins, so people could buy on a shoestring. And when they began pulling the plug . . . you had a deluge of weakness. You also had short-selling and a lack of rules.

Anything went, and everything did go.

short-selling
to sell stocks without having them in one's possession at the time of the sale; the seller hoped that when it came time to deliver the shares, the price of the stock would have gone down and he could buy it again

—From Studs Terkel, Hard Times: An Oral History of the Great Depression. *New York: The Free Press, 1986.*

President Hoover Explains the Crash

On December 3, 1929, President Hoover addressed the Congress in his annual State of the Union message. Herbert Hoover came to the presidency on the Republican ticket in 1928 after gaining fame for his humanitarian work during and after World War I. Before becoming president, Hoover had been the secretary of commerce (1920–1928). He was a skilled manager and cared deeply about human suffering. Hoover optimistically believed that the Depression was only a temporary emergency. The following account is how he explained the stock market crash and its impact.

THE COUNTRY HAS ENJOYED a large degree of prosperity and sound progress during the past year. . . . The long upward trend of fundamental progress, however, gave rise to over-optimism as to profits, which translated itself into a wave of uncontrolled speculation in securities, resulting in the diversion of capital from business to the stock market and the inevitable crash. The natural consequences have been a reduction in the consumption of luxuries and semi-necessities by those who

"The long upward trend . . . gave rise to over-optimism."

securities
stocks and bonds

have met with losses, and a number of persons thrown temporarily out of employment.

—*From President Herbert Hoover's First Annual State of the Union message, December 3, 1929, in* The State of the Union Messages of the Presidents, 1905–1966, *Fred L. Israel, editor. New York: Chelsea House, 1966.*

THINK ABOUT THIS

1. According to the president, how did "over-optimism" about potential profits lead to the Crash?
2. What might Hoover have meant by "fundamental progress"?
3. Would you have been alarmed if you had heard the president's speech?

A Life Turned Upside Down

By 1930, hundreds of businesses were closing and laying off their workers. Banks began to fail after customers rushed to withdraw their cash. The December 11, 1930, closing of the Bank of the United States in New York City—with deposits of $200 million—was the most notable failure. The bank closings took away the life savings of ordinary men and women, who had come to view the financial institutions as safe places for their hard-earned dollars.

In the following excerpt, Diana Morgan recounts how the collapse of her well-to-do family's finances changed her life. Diana's father was a North Carolina cotton merchant who also owned a general store. When the Depression hit, his customers—local farmers and townspeople—lost their farms and jobs and could

As the economy declined rapidly into chaos, Americans rushed to withdraw money from their savings accounts, forcing banks out of business. By the end of 1930, more than 1,300 U.S. banks had closed their doors; three years later, the number had skyrocketed to 4,000.

no longer shop at his store. Eventually, he lost the store and went bankrupt.

THE BANKS FAILED about the time I was getting ready to go to college. My family thought of my going to Wellesley, Vassar, Smith [prestigious women's schools in the Northeast]—but we had so little money, we thought of a school in North Carolina. It wasn't so expensive.

It was in my junior year, and I came home for Christmas. . . . I found the telephone disconnected. . . . We didn't have a cook any more, we didn't have a cleaning woman. . . . The first thing I noticed . . . was that my great-grandfather's house was lost, about to be sold for taxes. Our own house was sold. . . . for $5,000 in back taxes. I was born in that house. I never felt so old in my life as I felt the first two years of college. 'Cause I hadn't found a new life for myself, and the other one was finished.

"I never felt so old in my life."

—*From Studs Terkel,* Hard Times: An Oral History of the Great Depression. *New York: The Free Press, 1986.*

THINK ABOUT THIS

1. Why was a wealthy family like Morgan's affected by the Depression?

2. How might her family's financial collapse have affected others in her community?

Under the Shadow of the Hawk, Gordon Parks' Story

For many Americans, the stock market crash of 1929 had little or no meaning. They owned no shares, had little or no savings, and were accustomed to scraping by as farmers, sharecroppers, or laborers. These were the "old poor," and the Depression just meant more of the same. Some, however, did have hopes and plans for the future, and among them was a young African American named Gordon Parks. For him, the Crash meant a sudden and rude detour.

In the following selection, Parks recalls the events of 1929. Parks was born in Fort Scott, Kansas, in 1912 and left home at age sixteen to live with his sister in Saint Paul, Minnesota. For a while, he worked part-time as a bellboy in an exclusive club for the city's wealthy businessmen. Gordon Parks eventually became a world-famous photographer, filmmaker, writer, and poet.

BY SEPTEMBER I HAD SAVED a little money, received a two-dollar raise and fallen . . . in love; and on the ninth day of that same month I enrolled at Central High School. Working evenings and weekends at the club, I overheard talk of Hoover, A.T.&T., General Motors, U.S. Steel, General Electric, the Federal Reserve Bank and other such names. And though I didn't know what the conversations really meant, I sensed a certain optimism in them.

On the fifteenth of October, I asked Sally [his girlfriend] if she would marry me. She only blushed, laughed and explained, "Why . . . I must finish high school before thinking about such things." I felt a little crushed; but she hadn't refused outright. Furthermore, common sense warned me to finish high school too. . . . I opened a savings account, anticipating the day, a year later, when we would both graduate.

The employees' locker room at the club was unusually quiet when I arrived at work one Wednesday that same month. Waiters who had known each other for years were sitting about as though they were strangers. The cause for silence was tacked to the bulletin board. It read: "Because of unforeseen circumstances, some personnel will be laid off the first of next month. Those directly affected will be notified in due time."

"That Hoover's ruining the country," an old waiter finally said. No one answered him. I changed into my suit of blue tails, wondering what had happened.

By Thursday the entire world knew. "Market Crashes—Panic Hits Nation!" one headline blared. The newspapers were full of it, and I read everything I could get my hands on, gathering in the full meaning of such terms as Black Thursday, deflation and depression. I couldn't imagine such financial disaster touching my small world; it surely concerned only the rich. But by the first week of November I too knew differently; along with millions of others across the nation, I was without a job. All that next week I searched for any kind of work that would prevent my leaving school. Again it was, "We're firing, not hiring." "Sorry, sonny, nothing doing here." Finally, on the seventh of November I went to school and cleaned out my locker, knowing it was impossible to stay on. A piercing chill was in the air as I walked back to the rooming house. The hawk had come. I could already feel his wings shadowing me.

"Sorry, sonny, nothing doing here."

—*From Gordon Parks,* A Choice of Weapons. *New York: Harper & Row, 1965.*

Think about This

1. What did Gordon do to plan for the future?

2. In what ways do you think the Crash affected Parks?

3. What do you think the hawk stands for?

"Brother, Can You Spare a Dime?"

E. Y. Harburg, nicknamed "Yip," was a businessman who wrote verse as a hobby. When the stock market crashed, he, like thou-

Long lines on city streets were a common sight during the Depression. People waited their turn, hoping to find food for their families or a job to pay their bills. Often they waited for nothing—there simply wasn't enough food or work to go around.

sands of others, was thrown out of work. Cut off from his previous life, Harburg decided to devote himself to writing songs. His later work appeared in such Broadway shows as *Finian's Rainbow* and the movie classic *The Wizard of Oz.*

Harburg wrote the lyrics for the song "Brother, Can You Spare a Dime?" in 1932, as part of the Broadway show *New Americana.* He was inspired by the sight of jobless men waiting in breadlines for free food or begging on the street for small change. Many were veterans of World War I, who had worked hard and were looking forward to a good life. Then came the Crash. Harburg's song follows. In 1932, a dime could buy a donut. A nickel bought a cup of coffee.

They used to tell me
I was building a dream.
And so I followed the mob,
When there was earth to plow,
Or guns to bear,
I was always there
Right on the job.
They used to tell me
I was building a dream,
With peace and glory ahead,
Why should I be standing in line,
Just waiting for bread?

Once I built a railroad,
I made it run,
Made it race against time.
Once I built a railroad;
Now it's done.
Brother, can you spare a dime?
Once I built a tower up to the sun,
Brick, and rivet, and lime;
Once I built a tower,
Now it's done.
Brother, can you spare a dime?

Once in khaki suits,
Gee, we looked swell,
Full of that Yankee Doodle-de-dum.
Half a million boots went sloggin' through Hell,
And I was the kid with the drum.

Say, don't you remember?
They called me Al.
It was Al all the time.
Why don't you remember?
I'm your pal.
Say Buddy, can you spare a dime?

"Say, don't you remember?"

—From "Brother, Can You Spare a Dime?" Words by E. Y. Harburg, music by Jay Gorney. © Copyright 1932 by Warner Bros. (renewed).

THINK ABOUT THIS

1. What makes this song so powerful and sad?

2. How would you describe the state of mind of the character in the song? Disillusioned, angry, cynical, depressed?

Letter from a "Forgotten Man"

President Hoover was staunchly opposed to "big government." He felt that it was not the role of the federal government to become involved in providing relief to those hurt by the Depression. That responsibility, he thought, lay with local governments and privately funded charities. To help revive the economy, he urged businesses to hire workers and expand production. He also called on farmers to plant fewer crops and thus avoid flooding the market and pushing crop prices lower. Hoover did establish a government agency to spur economic activity, however. This was the Reconstruction Finance Corporation (RFC), created in 1932. The RFC arranged for a loan of $1.5 billion to save banks and businesses. Funds were also paid out to help those on the brink of losing their homes.

Despite Hoover's efforts, the economy fell into a steep, steady decline. People still could find no work, the poor got hungrier, and crop prices continued to drop. Many Americans believed he and the government weren't doing enough to help them. The following letter was written to the president by an unemployed worker from Pottstown, Pennsylvania.

October 30, 1930

Dear Sir:

I am persuaded to write you, concerning aid to unemployment. I hope this movement will be speeded up so people in Pottstown will feel and know the results before cold weather comes upon us. . . . It really is alarming that this so called prosperous nation . . . must suffer [on account] of a few men seeking power and . . . have laws [passed] to suit themselves. . . . I am one of the men out of work but the rich don't care so long as they have full and plenty.

> *" . . . the rich don't care so long as they have full and plenty."*

I hope relief will be coming soon and some action [taken]. . . . The people have been [lied to so often] that you cannot believe anything only what you can see. I hope that Wall St will never have the power again to cause such a panic upon the people.

—*From* Down and Out in the Great Depression: Letters from the Forgotten Man, *Robert S. McElvaine, editor. Chapel Hill, NC: University of North Carolina Press, 1983.*

1. What does the writer want?

2. Whom does he blame for the crisis? Do you think he is correct to blame them?

3. What do you think he thought of Hoover?

Scrounging for Work on the San Francisco Waterfront

As businesses closed and employees were laid off, more and more workers competed for fewer and fewer jobs. Men left their families to search for work. In the following excerpt, Ed Paulsen recalls what it was like being a recent high school graduate in 1930. He left his South Dakota home and traveled through the West doing odd jobs. After a few months he found himself in San Francisco looking for work on the docks. This is how he describes the "shape up" at the docks. (During a shape-up, a company foreman picks and chooses workers for the day from a group of men who jostle with one another to be noticed and given work.)

Pinkerton cops
security men hired by the company

hole
area inside of a cargo ship where raw goods are stored

I'D GET UP AT FIVE IN THE MORNING and head for the waterfront. Outside the Spreckles Sugar Refinery . . . there would be a thousand men. You know dang well there's only three or four jobs. The guy [hiring boss] would come out with two little Pinkerton cops: "I need two guys . . . to go into the hole." A thousand men would fight like . . . dogs to get through there.

Skid Row
a place where jobless men would gather

So you'd drift up to Skid Row. There'd be thousands of men there. Guys . . . making weird speeches, phony theories on economics. About eleven-thirty, the real leaders would take over. They'd say: O.K., we're going to City Hall. . . . We'd shout around the steps.

I remember the demands: We demand work, we demand shelter . . . we demand groceries. . . . I remember . . . how courageous this seemed to me . . . because you knew that society wasn't going to give it to you. . . . There was nothing coming. . . . These were fathers, eighty percent of them. They had held jobs and didn't want to kick society to pieces. They just wanted to go to work.

"They just wanted to go to work."

We weren't talking revolution; we were talking jobs.

—*From Studs Terkel,* Hard Times: An Oral History of the Great Depression. *New York: The Free Press, 1986.*

THINK ABOUT THIS

1. What did the men described here do if they did not succeed in getting work at the docks for the day?

2. What does the writer mean by the word "revolution"? Why might someone think these men wanted to revolt?

3. If these men did want a revolution, whom might they revolt against? Can you think of a time when such a revolution occurred, either in America or in another part of the world?

A Senator Blames a "Bankrupt" Leadership

Robert LaFollette, Jr., a U.S. senator from Wisconsin, wrote the following article for *The Nation* magazine in 1931. He attacks the

Hoover administration and its philosophy of "rugged individualism," words Hoover used in a 1928 campaign speech. According to Hoover, the success of the American system was based on the concepts of ordered liberty, equal opportunity, self-reliance, and individual initiative. Hoover, like many other Americans, felt the government should stay outside the lives of citizens. LaFollette clearly did not agree.

FOR EIGHTEEN MONTHS, unemployment has been spreading poverty and . . . suffering through industrial and agricultural areas alike. No one yet knows when the present economic disaster will be brought to an end. . . . The third winter of unemployment is approaching. Responsibility for the failure of the federal government to provide a program for the relief of distress among millions of our people rests squarely upon President Hoover. The bankruptcy of his leadership in the worst economic crisis in our history reveals the tragic failure of rugged individualism.

A caricature of President Herbert Hoover, whom many accused of turning a cold shoulder to the American people.

—From The Nation, *July 15, 1931.*

1. How would you describe LaFollette's tone in this article?
2. Why did the senator think the philosophy of "rugged individualism" was a failure?

The Emergence of FDR

On May 22, 1932, presidential hopeful Franklin Delano Roosevelt was given an honorary degree by Oglethorpe University in Georgia and addressed the graduating class. In his speech, Roosevelt demanded a radical response to the nation's economic crisis. Excerpts from his speech follow.

THE YEAR 1928 DOES NOT seem far in the past, but since that time . . . the world about us has experienced significant changes. Four years ago . . . you could expect to take your place in a society well supplied with material things and could look forward to . . . living in your own homes, each . . . with a two-car garage; and, without great effort, would be providing yourselves and your families with all the necessities and amenities of life.

How sadly different is the picture which we see around us today! If only the mirage [of prosperity] had vanished, we should not complain. . . . But with it have vanished, not only the easy gains of speculation, but much of the savings of thrifty and prudent men and women. . . . More calamitous still, there has vanished . . . the certainty of today's bread and clothing.

You have been struck, I know, by the tragic irony of our economic situation today. We have not been brought to our present state by any natural calamity. . . . We have a superabundance of raw materials, a more than ample supply of equipment for manufacturing these materials into goods . . . and transportation and commercial facilities for making them available to all who need them. But raw materials stand unused, factories stand idle, railroad traffic continues to dwindle, merchants sell less and less, while millions of able-bodied men and women . . . are clamoring for the opportunity to work. This is the awful paradox with which we are confronted.

"The millions who are in want will not stand by silently forever."

The country needs and . . . demands bold, persistent experimentation. It is common sense to take a method and try it. If it fails, admit it frankly and try another. But above all, try something. The millions who are in want will not stand by silently forever.

—From Address at Oglethorpe University, May 22, 1932, in
The Works of Franklin D. Roosevelt. *Available at the New Deal Network*
Web site: http://newdeal.feri.org/speeches/1932d.htm

THINK ABOUT THIS

1. What did graduates have to look forward to in 1928? In 1932?

2. What point was Roosevelt making about "easy money" versus thrift and prudence?

3. What does he mean by the "tragic irony" of the economy, and what is his prescription for a cure?

Veterans Try to Collect a Benefit

Unemployed men who had fought in World War I decided to march on Washington in 1932 to demand the payment of a bonus promised to them by the federal government. The bonus was not to be paid until 1945, but the veterans wanted—and needed—it immediately. They formed what came to be known

Composed of World War I veterans, the Bonus Army descended on Washington in the spring of 1932, demanding that the government immediately pay out the bonus promised to all who had fought in the war. By the end of their protest, the men had been driven from the nation's capital. "We were heroes in 1917," said one veteran, "but we're bums now."

as the Bonus Army. Starting out on May 11 in Portland, Oregon, the bonus marchers made their way across the country by rail. They arrived in Washington, D.C., eighteen days later. Other jobless men soon joined the group, many with their families. By mid-June, about 20,000 veterans camped at the outskirts of Washington.

President Hoover refused to meet with the bonus marchers or discuss their demands. He regarded them as hoodlums and political radicals intent on bringing about a revolution. In July, Hoover ordered the U.S. Army to break up the group. The following is a description of what happened next. Jim Sheridan, the narrator here, was not a veteran member of the Bonus Army but chose to travel with it as it progressed across the country.

WHEN WE GOT TO WASHINGTON, there was quite a few ex-servicemen there before us. There was no arrangements for housing. Most of the men that had wives and children were living in Hooverville. This was across the Potomac River—what was known as Anacostia Flats. . . .

They had come to petition Hoover, to give them the bonus before it was due. And Hoover refused this. He told them they couldn't get it because it would make the country go broke. They would hold midnight vigils around the White House and march around [it] in shifts.

They were ordered out [of Washington] four or five times, and they refused. The police chief was called to send them out, but he refused. I also heard that the marine commander . . . also refused. Finally, the one they did get to shove these bedraggled

Hooverville
one of many shantytowns across the United States that were ironically named for the president

It wasn't only the Bonus Marchers who took up residence in Hoovervilles. Families around the country lost their homes when they couldn't pay their mortgage or their rent. With no place to go, they had no choice but to seek another form of shelter, often in miserable shanties like these.

ex-servicemen out of Washington was . . . [Douglas] MacArthur. He was riding a white horse. Behind him were tanks, troops of the regular army.

When these ex-soldiers wouldn't move, they'd poke them with their bayonets, and hit them on the head with the butt of a rifle. . . . They managed to get them out. . . . As night fell, they [the Bonus Army] crossed the Potomac. They were given orders to get out of Anacostia Flats, and they refused. The soldiers set those shanties on fire. They were practically smoked out. I saw it from a distance. I could see the pandemonium. The soldiers threw tear gas at them. . . . It was one assignment they reluctantly took on. They were younger than the marchers. It was like sons attacking their fathers.

"The soldiers threw tear gas at them."

And so the bonus marchers straggled back to the various places they came from. And without their bonus.

—*From Studs Terkel,* Hard Times: An Oral History of the Great Depression. *New York: The Free Press, 1986.*

THINK ABOUT THIS

1. Was Hoover wrong to withhold the bonuses?

2. How would you have reacted to the Bonus March if you had been a World War I veteran? Would you have participated in it or criticized it?

Chapter 2

A Bold Experiment Begins

PRESIDENT HOOVER TOLD AMERICANS to remain optimistic, and business leaders urged consumers to spend to boost business and help morale. Yet Americans were unable to find work. Without money to buy food or pay rent, many became homeless. In rural areas families took to living in tents, even in the winter. In open lots in and around cities, men eked out an existence in the ramshackle wood and tin huts of the Hoovervilles. The economic system appeared broken and the nation's leadership incapable of putting it back together. While some Americans blamed themselves for their misfortune, others blamed Herbert Hoover. As the Depression continued, people began to lose hope.

In the election of 1932, voters overwhelmingly rejected Hoover's bid for a second term and chose Franklin Delano Roosevelt, former governor of New York, who ran as the Democratic Party's candidate. In his nomination acceptance speech, FDR promised to deliver a "new deal for the American people." What the new deal meant remained to be seen.

The Democratic National Convention, 1932: As the presidential election drew near, most Americans were looking for a change in leadership. Blaming Herbert Hoover for the nation's sorrowful state, many turned to Democratic candidate Franklin D. Roosevelt, who proposed bold ideas to improve the economy.

Roosevelt came from a wealthy New York family. He was a cousin of former president Theodore Roosevelt and was married to Theodore's niece, Eleanor. Raised in upper-class surroundings on an estate in Hyde Park, Roosevelt chose to devote himself to politics. His rise was rapid: he served first in the New York State Assembly, then as assistant secretary of the navy, and then ran unsuccessfully as the vice presidential candidate in 1920. When stricken with polio in 1921, Roosevelt lost the use of his legs, but none of his ambition and drive. He continued to pursue political office and was elected governor of New York in 1928. Four years later he became president of the United States during one of its darkest periods.

Roosevelt had promised Americans that he would do something to solve the crisis—and he did. During his first one hundred days in office, Congress passed an abundance of the legislation he requested. Collectively, the programs born of this legislation were called the New Deal. You'll read about several New Deal programs and how people reacted to them in the selections that follow.

The First Inaugural Address of FDR

Franklin Delano Roosevelt won a landslide victory in the presidential election of 1932. He was sworn in as president of the United States on March 4, 1933. In this, his first inaugural address, FDR showed not only compassion for the American people and a promise of vigorous national leadership, but also a great spirit. His words "the only thing we have to fear is fear itself" gave heart to millions and are among the most famous in American history.

THIS IS . . . THE TIME TO SPEAK the truth, the whole truth, frankly and boldly. Nor need we shrink from honestly facing conditions in our country today. This great Nation will endure as it has endured, will revive and will prosper. So, first of all, let me assert my firm belief that the only thing we have to fear is fear itself. . . .

In such a spirit on my part and on yours we face our common difficulties. . . . Values have shrunken to fantastic levels; taxes have risen; our ability to pay has fallen; government of all kinds is faced by serious curtailment of income; . . . farmers find no markets for their produce; the savings of many years in thousands of families are gone.

More important, a host of unemployed citizens face the grim problem of existence, and an equally great number toil with little return. . . .

This Nation asks for action, and action now.

" . . . the only thing we have to fear is fear itself."

Our greatest primary task is to put people to work. . . . It can be accomplished in part by direct recruiting by the Government itself, treating the task as we would treat the emergency of war, but at the same time, through this employment, accomplishing greatly needed projects to stimulate and reorganize the use of our natural resources. . . .

I am prepared under my constitutional duty to recommend the measures that a stricken Nation in the midst of a stricken world may require. These measures . . . I shall seek, within my constitutional authority, to bring to speedy adoption.

In the event that the national emergency is still critical, I shall not evade the clear course of duty that will then confront me. I shall ask the Congress for . . . broad Executive power to wage a war against the emergency, as great as the power that would be given to me if we were in fact invaded by a foreign foe.

—From *Inaugural Address, March 4, 1933, in* Works of Franklin D. Roosevelt. *Available at the New Deal Network Web site: http://newdeal.feri.org/speeches/1933a.htm*

THINK ABOUT THIS

1. What will be the first task of FDR's administration?
2. Would a listener expect the powers of the executive branch of the federal government to change under the new president?

A Fireside Chat

In the 1930s practically every household in the United States had a radio. President Roosevelt understood the power of this medium and used it regularly to communicate his policies to the American people. He called his radio talks "fireside chats." In the following excerpt from his first talk, delivered from the White House on March 12, 1933, the president explains why he has called for a bank holiday. He had no choice. In February, the governor of Michigan had ordered the banks in his state closed for eight days. He called the closing a "bank holiday" but there was nothing festive about the event. Such closings were desperate measures to keep the banks from collapsing. When the Michigan banks closed, panic spread to other states. Soon people were rushing to their local banks and taking out their money, stuffing it in mattresses, under carpets, and in tin cans. In light of such events, FDR called for a national bank holiday.

Banks began to reopen on March 13 in a new atmosphere. They were placed under government supervision and the amount of gold and currency flowing out of them was strictly regulated. Depositors began to look at the banks as safe places for their money. Following is an excerpt from FDR's chat on the bank crisis.

Roosevelt delivers a "fireside chat" from the study in his home in Hyde Park, New York.

I WANT TO TALK FOR A FEW MINUTES with the people of the United States about banking. . . . I want to tell you what has been done in the last few days, why it was done, and what the next steps are going to be.

First of all let me state the simple fact that when you deposit money in a bank the bank does not put the money into a safe-deposit vault. It invests your money in many different forms of credit-bonds, commercial paper, mortgages and many other kinds of loans. In other words, the bank puts your money to work to keep the wheels of industry and of agriculture turning around. A comparatively small part of the money you put into the bank is kept in currency. . . .

" . . . scarcely a bank in the country was open to do business."

What, then, happened during the last few days of February and the first few days of March? Because of undermined confidence on the part of the public, there was a general rush by a large portion of our population to turn bank deposits into currency or gold . . . a rush so great that the soundest banks could not get enough currency to meet the demand. . . . It was . . . impossible to sell perfectly sound assets of a bank and convert them into cash except at panic prices far below their real value.

By the afternoon of March 3, scarcely a bank in the country was open to do business. Proclamations temporarily closing them in whole or in part had been issued by the governors in almost all the states.

It was then that I issued the proclamation providing for the nation-wide bank holiday, and this was the first step in the Government's reconstruction of our financial and economic fabric.

—From "On the Bank Crisis," March 12, 1933, from Fireside Chats of Franklin D. Roosevelt. Available at the Franklin D. Roosevelt Presidential Library and Museum Web site: http://www.fdrlibrary.marist.edu/031233.html

1. Why did people rush to withdraw their money from banks? What was the result of these "panic" withdrawals?

2. Why could the banks not immediately convert their assets into cash?

3. What government regulation exists today to assure people of the safety of their bank deposits?

FDR Calls for Relief for the Jobless

One of the first actions taken by the Roosevelt administration was relief for the unemployed. There were about 15 million people without work in 1933. States and cities were unable to provide help to so many, and private charities had run out of funds. Even the Congress, which had set aside $300 million for aid in 1932, had exhausted its funds. In this speech, delivered on March 21, 1933, FDR gives an overview of his plan.

"I propose to create a civilian conservation corps."

TO THE CONGRESS:

It is essential to our recovery program that measures immediately be enacted aimed at unemployment relief. A direct attack in this problem suggests three types of legislation.

The first is the enrollment of workers now by the Federal Government for such public employment as can be quickly started.

The second is grants to States for relief work.

The third extends to a broad public works labor-creating program.

I propose to create a civilian conservation corps to be used in simple work not interfering with normal employment, and confining itself to forestry, the prevention of soil erosion, flood control, and similar projects.

Control and direction of such work can be carried on by existing machinery of the departments of Labor, Agriculture, War and Interior.

I estimate that 250,000 men can be given temporary employment by early summer if you give me authority to proceed within the next two weeks.

—*From* The Public Papers and Addresses of Franklin D. Roosevelt, *Vol. 2, 1933, New York: Random House, 1938, p. 80. Also available at the New Deal Network Web site: http://newdeal.feri.org/speeches/1933c.htm*

THINK ABOUT THIS

In his inaugural address, FDR had promised to "put people to work." In an earlier speech, to the graduating class at Oglethorpe University, he had advocated "bold, persistent experimentation." Do you think he was true to his word?

The CCC Is Formed

The Civilian Conservation Corps (CCC), established in March 1933, was one of the first and most successful of the New Deal programs. It gave work to hundreds of thousands of young men aged eighteen to twenty-five. CCC workers were organized like an army and were put to work in a variety of ways. They planted trees in national parks, blazed trails, and built roads. They also constructed lodges to attract visitors to places of great natural beauty, such as Timberline Lodge, at the base of Mount Hood in Oregon. They planted grasses on eroded hillsides and dug irrigation ditches in arid regions. The CCC employed about three

Workers in the Civilian Conservation Corps, a New Deal agency, fight a fire in Idaho's Challis National Forest, 1937.

million men during its nine years of existence. For many of these men, it provided an opportunity to continue their education and learn self-discipline. In the following selection, Robert L. Miller recalls what being part of the CCC meant to him. He was in his early twenties when he joined.

THERE IS NO NEED TO MENTION MUCH of my life before I enrolled in the Civilian Conservation Corps. . . . I was often hungry, and almost constantly broke.

When I finally enrolled in this great enterprise at Sacramento,

California, in October, 1933, I was conscious of just one thing—I would be fed, clothed and sheltered during the coming winter. Also I would receive enough actual cash each month to provide the few luxuries I desired.

The two weeks I had to wait between the time I enrolled and the day we were to leave for camp were given over to much thinking. . . . Several questions flashed through my mind. Would I make friends with my fellow members? What kind of work would I be doing? Would I be able to "take it"? This last question was by far the most important to me.

Let me pause for a moment to give you a short character analysis of myself. For years . . . I could not overcome the feeling that I was just a little inferior to my fellow men. I did not credit myself with the quality of a leader among men. . . . It was in this frame of mind that I joined seventy other young men on the morning of October 26, to leave for our camp in the Sierra Nevada Mountains. . . .

Early in November we moved to our winter camp near Hayward, California. During the period of camp construction that followed our move, I was put in charge of several small jobs. They were insignificant in their nature, but it did me a lot of good just to think that I was considered reliable enough to boss even a small project. . . .

"It gave me a chance to stand on my own two feet."

[Several months] later news came to camp that an Educational Advisor was coming to camp to direct the boys in their pursuit of education. Also we heard that some man in camp was to be appointed to the newly created position of Assistant Educational Advisor. This new position was to carry an assistant leader's rating, which meant a raise in pay. . . . On April 6, our Educational Advisor arrived in camp, and that evening I was told I had been appointed his assistant. My goal had been reached. . . .

I shall try to convey to you just what the Civilian Conservation Corps has meant to me. . . . First of all, by enrolling in President

Roosevelt's peace-time army, I managed to retain my self respect. I did not have to become either a parasite, living off my relatives, or a professional bum. It gave me a chance to stand on my own two feet and make my own way in the world. Then it gave me the opportunity to make friendships that will live forever.

—From Robert L. Miller, "It's a Great Life," in National Archives and Records Administration, Record Group 35, Division of Selection, Success Stories, 1937. Available at the New Deal Network Web site: http://newdeal.feri.org/ccc/ccc009.htm

THINK ABOUT THIS

1. What personal goals did Miller hope to achieve in the CCC?

2. Why do you think he was selected for a leadership role?

3. The CCC was abolished in 1942. Do you think such an organization might have value today?

TVA—Rebuilding a Region

The Tennessee Valley Authority (TVA) was one of the largest and most controversial projects of the New Deal. The TVA came into being on May 18, 1933. Its purpose was to bring flood control and electricity to the people living in the Tennessee River basin. The region, which is approximately 41,000 square miles in area, includes parts of Tennessee, Kentucky, Virginia, North Carolina, Georgia, Alabama, and Mississippi. A series of dams, which produced electricity, and reservoirs were constructed on land taken over by the federal government. The long-range goals of the TVA were the improvement of agriculture and the industrialization of

To control water resources in the Tennessee River basin, the TVA constructed a series of dams across a 650-mile stretch of land.

this economically depressed region. The Tennessee Valley Authority still exists.

Opponents of the TVA believed that it was not the role of the federal government to be involved in developing and distributing electrical power. They held that such an enterprise put the government in competition with private utility companies, whose role it should be. Some people also argued that projects like the TVA would bring the United States a step closer to a state-planned economy like that found under communism in the Soviet Union. The government of the Soviet Union owned the means of production, deciding what, how, and when to produce a commodity and how much to charge for it. Free and open competition did not exist under the Soviet system.

Excerpts from the Tennessee Valley Authority Act follow.

BE IT ENACTED BY THE SENATE and House of Representatives of the United States of America in Congress assembled, that for the purpose of maintaining and operating the properties now owned by the United States in the vicinity of Muscle Shoals, Alabama, in the interest of the national defense and for agriculture and industrial development, and to improve navigation in the Tennessee River and to control the destructive flood waters in the Tennessee River and Mississippi River Basins, there is hereby created a body corporate by the name of "Tennessee Valley Authority" (hereinafter referred to as the "Corporation"). . . .

"The President shall . . . recommend to Congress such legislation as he deems proper . . . for the economic and social well-being of the people."

The board of directors of the Corporation . . . shall be composed of three members, to be appointed by the President, by and with the advice and consent of the Senate. In appointing the members of the board, the President shall designate the chairman. All other officials, agents, and employees shall be designated and selected by the board. . . .

The board . . . shall have power to acquire real estate for the construction of dams, reservoirs, transmission lines, power houses, and other structures, and navigation projects at any point along the Tennessee River, or any of its tributaries, and in the event that the owner or owners of such property shall fail and refuse to sell to the Corporation at a price deemed fair and reasonable by the board, then the Corporation may proceed to exercise the right of eminent domain, and to condemn all property that it deems necessary for carrying out the purposes of this Act.

The President shall, from time to time . . . recommend to Congress such legislation as he deems proper to carry out . . . for the economic and social well-being of the people living in said river basin.

—*From Tennessee Valley Authority Act, May 18, 1933. Available at the New Deal Network Web site: http://newdeal.feri.org/acts/us07.htm*

The law of eminent domain—the right of the government to take over private property for public use—is based on the belief that the government, representing the welfare of the people as a whole, has greater power than the individual. According to the law, the government must pay the individual owner a fair price for the property taken. If the owner refuses to sell, the government may "condemn" the land and have a fair price determined by an appraiser, which the owner must accept. Do you think that the law of eminent domain is fair?

Lorena Hickok Reports

Lorena Hickok was a former journalist who worked for Harry Hopkins, the head of the Federal Emergency Relief Administration (FERA) and a close adviser to President Roosevelt. FERA coordinated the federal government's assistance to the states to help the jobless. Hopkins asked Hickok to be his confidential investigator and gather information about the everyday lives of those affected by the Depression. Hopkins wanted to know everything, the bad as well as the good. For more than two years, Lorena Hickok traveled across thirty states and reported to him on what she saw. The following letter recounts Hickok's impression of the Tennessee River Valley and the changes brought about by the TVA.

Florence, Alabama June 6, 1934

Dear Mr. Hopkins:

    A Promised Land, bathed in golden sunlight, is rising out of the grey shadows of want and squalor and wretchedness down here in the Tennessee Valley these days.

Ten thousand men are at work, building with timber and steel and concrete the New Deal's most magnificent project.

Thousands of them are residents of the Valley, working five and a half hours a day, five days a week, for a really LIVING wage. Houses are going up for them to live in—better houses than they have ever had in their lives before. And in their leisure time they are studying— farming, trades, the art of living, preparing themselves for the fuller lives they are to lead in that Promised Land. . . .

With TVA getting up standards in rehabilitation, the rest of the state has got a long, long way to go.

Out of nearly 70,000 families on relief in Tennessee, probably 30,000 or more live in small towns or in the country. Many of these are in abandoned lumber and mining camps. Most of them who are farmers apparently are living on submarginal or marginal land.

Fairly typical . . . was a district I visited yesterday. Table land. Thin soil. Terrible housing. Illiteracy. Evidence of prolonged undernourishment. No knowledge of how to live decently or farm profitably if they had decent land.

On the job: the TVA gave thousands of impoverished Tennessee Valley residents the chance to earn a decent wage.

"Five years is about as long as you can get any crop on this land," one farmer told me. "Then it's gone and you have to clear some more and start over again."

Crops grown on it are stunted. Corn . . . grows only about a third as tall there as it does in Iowa. They tell me it isn't even good timber land. Just a thin coating of soil over rock. A county agent said it might make good orchard land, but any farming operation there should be under skilled supervision with authority to make farmers do as they were told.

> *"A Promised Land . . . is rising out of the grey shadows of want and squalor."*

Eastern Tennessee is worse. . . . There you see . . . evidence of what happens when you cut timber off mountain sides and plant crops there. There are great "bald patches" of rock on those mountains!

What to do with these people makes a nice little problem. Whether to move them off—and, if so, where to put them—or, on table land, for instance, where with careful and authoritative supervision they might eke out a living, leave them there and take a chance on their being absorbed in the industries that should be attracted down here by the cheap power furnished by TVA.

—*From* One Third of a Nation: Lorena Hickok Reports on the Great Depression, *Richard Lowitt and Maurine Beasley, editors. Urbana, IL: University of Illinois Press, 1981.*

THINK ABOUT THIS

1. Throughout the Great Depression, there was a conflict of philosophies about the role of government. Should government play a powerful part in regulating business, agriculture, and people's personal lives? Or should it stay far away and let everyone freely go about their lives and jobs, no matter the social costs? How does Hickok's report reflect the attitude of the Roosevelt administration on this issue?

2. What particular words does she use that give us clues to her own feelings about the New Deal?

The National Industrial Recovery Act Takes Effect

On June 16, 1933, the U.S. Congress passed the National Industrial Recovery Act. This act established the National Recovery Administration (NRA), a government bureau intended to help business and industry. The NRA would enforce codes of fair business practices, which would be drawn up by representatives of companies within major industries. Although the codes were meant primarily to aid business and industry, (they allowed, for example, member companies to set the lowest prices that could be charged for products), they also addressed concerns of

A 1933 cartoon depicts the National Recovery Administration as beneficial to both employer and worker.

the working man. The codes set minimum wages and maximum hours, and they supported the right of workers to organize themselves into unions. Prior to the formation of the NRA, government had little say over business practices; companies could compete freely, whether for good or ill. With the NRA, the government assumed greater control over private industry.

During its brief life, the NRA was involved in the drawing up of more than five hundred codes of fair practice. Its symbol was the Blue Eagle, which businesses were urged to display in their offices and factories as a sign of their participation. Consumers were urged to do business only with those stores and shops that displayed the Blue Eagle. Opponents of the NRA called it authoritarian, and in 1935 the Supreme Court declared it unconstitutional. President Roosevelt ended the NRA shortly thereafter. Several sections of the National Industrial Recovery Act follow.

SEC. 1 A national emergency productive of widespread unemployment and disorganization of industry, which burdens interstate and foreign commerce, affects the public welfare, and undermines the standards of living of the American people, is hereby declared to exist. . . .

SEC. 3 Upon application to the President by one or more trade or industrial associations or groups, the President may approve a code or codes of fair competition for the trade or industry.

SEC. 7 . . . employees shall have the right to organize and bargain collectively [as groups of workers instead of individually] through representatives of their own choosing, and shall be free from the interference, restraint, or coercion of employers.

> *"A national emergency . . . is hereby declared to exist."*

—From *"U.S. Statutes at Large,"* Vol. XLVIII, p. 195, *in* Documents of American History. *Henry Steele Commager, editor. New York: Appleton-Century-Crofts, 1963.*

1. The National Recovery Act starts out by declaring that the nation was in a state of emergency. What significance did this statement have for the following sections of the law?

2. Why would employers be opposed to labor unions? Are unions still important today?

3. Why do you think the NRA had such a brief life span?

Huey Long: "Every Man a King"

FDR wasn't the only political leader with a plan to get the nation back on its feet. Huey Long, the powerful Democratic senator from Louisiana, was a one-time supporter of FDR, but thought that Roosevelt was not going far enough to change the nation's economic policies. He had his own program to help the country. It was called Share Our Wealth. Long called for the elimination of all personal wealth over $5 million and a government-guaranteed annual minimum income of $5,000 for each family. In addition, Long proposed old-age pensions, a program of public works, a minimum wage for workers, and a shorter work week. Huey Long gave a speech in the Senate on February 5, 1934, in which he described the Share Our Wealth program. Part of his speech is included here.

PEOPLE OF AMERICA: In every community get together at once and organize a share-our-wealth society—Motto: Every man a king.

"We have waited long enough."

An ardent enemy of big business and the wealthy, Huey Long took every opportunity to dominate the Senate floor and describe his vision for the country. The flamboyant speaker was senator for a brief three years before his assassination in 1935.

PRINCIPLES AND PLATFORM:

1. To limit poverty by providing that every deserving family shall share in the wealth of America for not less than one third of the average wealth, thereby to possess not less than $5,000 free of debt.
2. To limit fortunes to such a few million dollars as will allow the balance of the American people to share in the wealth and profits of the land.
3. Old-age pensions of $30 per month to persons over 60 years of age who do not earn as much as $1,000 per year or who possess less than $10,000 in cash or property, thereby to remove from the field of labor in times of unemployment those who have contributed their share to the public service.
4. To limit the hours of work to such an extent as to prevent overproduction and to give the workers of America some share in the recreations, conveniences, and luxuries of life.
5. To balance agricultural production with what can be sold and consumed according to the laws of God, which have never failed.
6. To care for the veterans of our wars.
7. Taxation to run the Government to be supported, first, by reducing big fortunes from the top, thereby to improve the country and provide employment in public works whenever agricultural surplus is such as to render unnecessary, in whole or in part, any particular crop.

SIMPLE AND CONCRETE—NOT AN EXPERIMENT

To share our wealth by providing for every deserving family to have one third of the average wealth would mean that . . . such a family could have a fairly comfortable home, an automobile, and a radio, with other reasonable home conveniences, and a place to educate their children. Through sharing the work, that is, by limiting the hours of toil so that all would share in what is made and produced in the land, every family would have enough coming in every year to feed, clothe, and provide a fair share of the luxuries of life to its members.

There would be no limit to opportunity. One might become a millionaire or more. There would be a chance for talent to make a man big, because enough would be floating in the land to give brains its chance to be used. As it is, no matter how smart a man may be, everything is tied up in so few hands that no amount of energy or talent has a chance to gain any of it.

Would it break up big concerns? No. It would simply mean that, instead of one man getting all the one concern made, that there might be 1,000 or 10,000 persons sharing in such excess fortune, any one of whom, or all of whom, might be millionaires and over.

I ask somebody in every city, town, village, and farm community of America to take this as my personal request to call a meeting of as many neighbors and friends as will come to it to start a share-our-wealth society. Elect a president and a secretary and charge no dues. The meeting can be held at a courthouse, in some town hall or public building, or in the home of someone.

"There should be every man a king in this land flowing with milk and honey instead of the lords of finance at the top and slaves and peasants at the bottom."

It does not matter how many will come to the first meeting. Get a society organized, if it has only two members. Then let us get to work quick, quick, quick to put an end by law to people starving and going naked in this land of too much to eat and too much to wear.

We have waited long enough for . . . financial masters to do these things. They have promised and promised. Now we find our country $10 billion further in debt on account of the depression, and big lenders even propose to get 90 percent of that out of the hides of the common people in the form of a sales tax.

There is nothing wrong with the United States. We have more food than we can eat. We have more clothes and things out of which to make clothes than we can wear. We have more houses and lands than the whole 120 million can use if they all had good homes. So what is the trouble? Nothing except that a handful of men have everything and the balance of the people have nothing if their debts were paid. There should be every man a king in this land flowing with milk and honey instead of the lords of finance at the top and slaves and peasants at the bottom.

—*From Senator Huey Long, speech before the Senate, February 5, 1934, advocating his Share Our Wealth program, Congressional Record, February 5, 1934. Available at the Social Security Administration Web site: www.ssa.gov/history/longsen.html*

THINK ABOUT THIS

1. In Long's opinion, who is responsible for the nation's plight? Why?

2. Long suggests that limits be placed on individual wealth. Does his idea correspond to traditional American ideals?

Families did what they could to get by during the Great Depression. For some this meant living out of a car and traveling the country in search of work. For others it meant humbly accepting relief from the government or charities. In such difficult times, simply having enough food to eat was often a luxury.

Chapter 3

Getting By
and Doing Without

THE GREAT DEPRESSION WAS A TIME when many Americans got by on very little money or did without the necessities of life. Wages fell from almost $25 per week in 1929 for manufacturing jobs to $16 per week for the same job in 1933. It was difficult to survive on these wages when, in 1933, bread sold for seven cents a loaf, eggs for twenty-nine cents a dozen, and milk for ten cents a quart. People who were out of work tried to find odd jobs such as mowing lawns or painting fences to get enough money to buy food. Many families planted vegetable gardens and ate what they were able to grow. In some very poor families, children took turns eating. People tried to help each other by giving away their leftover food to the needy. It was simply not enough, however, and even New Deal relief programs did not completely erase poverty from America. Accepting relief (as welfare was called in the 1930s) was degrading to many. The unemployed preferred to work instead of taking a government handout.

Many of the poor during the Depression were children. They had few or no toys and sometimes no food or clothing. Younger brothers and sisters wore their siblings' hand-me-down clothes. Many children had to work to help support their families. Child labor was common in the 1930s despite the Labor Standards Act of 1938, which set a minimum age of eighteen for dangerous occupations, sixteen for company jobs done during school hours, and fourteen for non-manufacturing jobs done after school hours. The money brought in by a young worker was often the difference between his or her family's eating or not. Many older children lied about their ages to get work. For employers, young workers were easy to hire and fire because no one expected them to speak out about poor treatment. They were also paid less than an adult worker.

Farmers were among the hardest hit by the Depression. Never rich, they lived from season to season, usually in debt to banks and loan holders for their livestock or farm machinery. When crops failed or natural disasters such as drought or tornadoes wiped out their efforts, they had no place to turn. Many of the farmers in the poorest regions of the United States became migrant laborers during the 1930s. Whole families traveled from region to region harvesting crops for a pittance. You'll read about how some Americans made do in the selections that follow.

"He Is Fixing to Foreclose Me": The Plight of the Farmers

Farmers suffered from economic hardship long before the stock market crash of 1929. Low prices for crops, years of drought, and continual debt placed the nation's small farmers in conditions of poverty or near-poverty before the hard times of the 1930s arrived. In the following letter to President Roosevelt, a Texas farmer explains his situation.

Sulphur Springs, Texas
December 11, 1934
President Roosevelt
Washington, D.C.

Dear President:

I am in debt needing help the worst in the world. I own my own little home and a few live stock . . . I have them all mortgaged to a man and he is fixing to foreclose me.

I have done all I could to pay the note and have failed on everything I've tried. I fell short on my crop this time and he didn't allow me even one nickel out of it to feed myself while I

> *"I am in debt needing help the worst in the world."*

was gathering it and now winter is here and I have a wife and three little children, haven't got clothes enough to hardly keep them from freezing. . . . We are in a suffering condition. My little children talking about Santa Claus and I hate to see Xmas come this time.

I have tried to compromise with the man that I am in debt to and he won't [accept] nothing but the money or my stock and I can't borrow the money and I need my stock so I am asking you for help of some kind please.

So I remain,

Your humble servant,
N.S.
P.S. That man won't even agree for me to have my stock fed.

—*From* Down and Out in the Great Depression: Letters from the Forgotten Man, *Robert S. McElvaine, editor. Chapel Hill, NC: University of North Carolina Press, 1983.*

1. After his crop "fell short," what did the farmer want his lender to do?

2. Do you think Roosevelt could help this man? If so, how?

"We Are Busy"—An Artist Gets Work at the WPA

The Work Projects Administration (WPA) was established in 1935 as part of FDR's New Deal. It was originally called the Works Progress Administration but was renamed in 1939. The WPA was headed by Harry Hopkins, and its goal was to provide jobs for the unemployed on public works projects. The WPA was responsible for thousands of building projects including roads, libraries, and airports. More than 8 million people were put to work by the WPA.

The Federal Art Project (FAP) was part of the WPA, as were the Federal Writers' Project and the Federal Theatre Project. Artists working under the FAP created murals for the nation's libraries, post offices, and courthouses. They also sculpted statues and ornamental figures for city parks. In return, the government paid them a salary of between $23 and $42 per week. The artists supplied their own materials whenever possible. By working for the FAP, artists survived and created beautiful art for the public. In the following excerpt, a San Francisco–based sculptor explains what the WPA meant to him.

LONG BEFORE THE WPA/FAP came into existence, I offered my services to several communities at day-labor wages if they would supply the materials and let me work. There must have been many artists with this same spirit. Movements like a government art project are not an accident; they come from great needs, the need of the artist to give something to the world as much as from his need to survive.

"We need artists."

We need artists who are interested in creating a universal culture. In being alive. In having something to say. And in saying it—ready to consider no sacrifice too great in making themselves heard. Artists who are concerned with universal truths. WPA/FAP has laid the foundation of a renaissance of art in America. It is the open sesame to a freer art and a more democratic use of the creations of the artist's hand and brain. It has freed American art. . . . For the present we have steel, stone, and tools. We have the spirit of great men and great cities to move us. We are busy.

Artist Lucia Wiley creates a mural for the Federal Art Project in 1940.

—From Beniamino Benvenuto Bufano, an essay written in 1936 for a proposed report to Congress on the value of the WPA/FAP in the file "Federal Support for the Visual Arts: the New Deal and Now," Library of the National Collection of Fine Arts of the Smithsonian Institution, Washington, D.C. Available at the New Deal Network Web site: http://newdeal.feri.org/art/art04.htm

1. According to the writer, why does an artist need to work?
2. What might this artist have meant by saying the FAP had made possible a freer, more democratic art?
3. Should the government support the creation of art, both in times of prosperity and during a depression?

Eleanor Roosevelt's Day at the Women's Handicraft Project

Eleanor Roosevelt was the eyes and ears of the president. She went places he could not and told him about what she learned. In the following excerpt from "My Day," her newspaper column, the first lady recalls a trip to the Milwaukee WPA Handicraft Project. Here, unemployed women made dolls, bookbindings, rugs, quilts, and other household items. The handicrafts were sold to schools, hospitals, and theaters for the cost of the materials. The project started in 1935 and employed five thousand before ending in 1943. The women who took part earned about $50 a month.

MY DAY: November 12, 1936, by Eleanor Roosevelt

I have just come back from one of the most interesting mornings I have ever spent. Milwaukee has a handicraft project for unskilled women. . . . They are doing artistic work under most able teachers. . . . These women have had few educational advantages and were so unskilled that they were rejected on the sewing project. . . . One woman made her own design for a piece of work which I much admired and she had had just three years in school.

They are binding scrap books for children; books to be used in hospitals; and books for the Braille project [for the blind]. . . . They [also] make rugs and hangings all of original design.

They are making dolls as attractive as any I have seen. . . . They are making costumes for public schools and institutions and the Municipal opera. . . . The schools provide the materials [and] two young people with art training who have not yet found jobs do the research and designs. The costumes remain as a permanent theatrical wardrobe in the schools or institutions to which they are sent.

"They are making dolls as attractive as any I have seen."

We visited a very fine sewing room for women where about nine hundred are employed. The working conditions are excellent and they have an opportunity to work on all types of modern machines, which is a help to future employment. Only five percent of the workers had any training before they entered this work room.

—From Eleanor Roosevelt, "My Day: November 12, 1936." Available at the New Deal Network Web site: http://newdeal.fer.org/dolls/md111236.htm

THINK ABOUT THIS

In what ways did the Handicraft Project help the women who participated?

A Clergyman Writes to the President

In 1935, FDR wrote a letter to the nation's clergy in which he asked them to report about conditions in their communities. The White House received hundreds of replies. Here a rabbi voices his thoughts to the president about the WPA and how it was working in his city.

Before the New Deal, people in need could turn only to private charities for help, and doing so could be a humiliating experience. Roosevelt believed that the government should take responsibility for its citizens, and helping people find work through the WPA was one way he found to do this.

Dear Mr. Roosevelt:

For about two years now I have been the supervisor of a project first in Work Relief and then under the Works Progress Administration. . . . This has brought me into direct contact with the very people for whom the . . . Works Program has been intended. I wish that those who are opposing such a program could meet these people[:] . . . old people who have worked hard all their lives, only to face desperate need in their old age; . . . middle-aged workers cast adrift not through their own incapability, but [that] of those who employed them; . . . young people who have just completed their education and find that the working world has no place for them. I have found some shirkers and cheaters, but they are a very small minority; and the thing that has impressed me is the eagerness with which the unemployed seek for work, even the most difficult.

As for the Works Program itself, I find that while it has been nobly conceived, it is often ineptly administered. . . . There is still great difficulty in fitting the right man to the job. I have sat for days at the central clearing offices, and know what I am talking about. Time

" . . . the thing that has impressed me is the eagerness with which the unemployed seek for work."

after time I have been sent people who are absolutely disqualified for my work, just because no one else knows what to do with them; while on the other hand, those for whom I asked and whom I knew would be both serviceable to me and happy in the work are the very ones that I have been unable to obtain.

In conclusion, a personal word. Do not be afraid of what is written by those who are afraid of change, . . . or by those who are offended because you do not act upon their own pet peeve. The masses of the people are still with you and you are their hope.

Yours sincerely,
Rabbi Simon Cohen
Brooklyn, NY

—From Letters from the Nation's Clergy, *October 27, 1935, FDR Library, President's Personal File, Entry 21, Box 22. Available at the New Deal Network Web site: http://newdeal.feri.org/cl015.htm*

THINK ABOUT THIS

1. In his work for the WPA, what has impressed the rabbi most?

2. What is his main criticism of the program?

A WPA Worker Complains

Not every person taking part in the WPA was happy with the program, especially when relief checks did not come on time. Here a man from Union City, New Jersey, seeks help from Harry Hopkins, who administered several of the New Deal's programs.

January 4, 1936

Dear Mr. Hopkins,

    I am writing to you because I am sick and tired of starving after I have done my share and worked in all kinds of weather for the money to feed and take care of my family. What I do earn is barely enough to keep us in food until the next check. Every check I get is so late that I am in debt up to my neck when it gets here and by the time I get through squareing up for what I owe for food and coal and medicine there isn't enough left for one decent meal. There are six in my family and their whole expense is on my check. . . . Can't you please do something about this?

    A Union City, New Jersey W.P.A. Worker,
    Thank you

—*From* Down and Out in the Great Depression: Letters from the Forgotten Man,
Robert S. McElvaine, editor. Chapel Hill, NC: University of North Carolina Press, 1983.

THINK ABOUT THIS

1. The writer doesn't give his name or full address. Why do you think he chose not to give Hopkins this information?

2. How do you think Hopkins felt about receiving a letter like this? Do you think he received positive letters as well?

High unemployment left thousands of families homeless, struggling to meet their most basic needs.

"I'd Rather Not Be on Relief"

Accepting relief in the form of welfare payments bothered many Americans. They were brought up to believe in the importance of self-reliance and hard work and wanted nothing more than a job. To many on relief, the payments were just too small to make much of a difference in their lives. They were still in poverty. The following song, written in 1938, is from the point of view of a migrant farmworker.

We go around all dressed in rags
While the rest of the world goes neat,
And we have to be satisfied
With half enough to eat.

"And we have to be satisfied With half enough to eat."

We have to live in lean-tos,
Or else we live in a tent,
For when we buy our bread and beans
There's nothing left for rent.

I'd rather not be on the rolls of relief,
Or work on the W.P.A.,
We'd rather work for the farmer
If the farmer could raise the pay;
Then the farmer could plant more cotton
And he'd get more money for spuds,
Instead of wearing patches,
We'd dress up in new duds.

—From *"I'd Rather Not Be on Relief,"* by Lester Hunter Shafter, in Voices from the Dust
Bowl: The Charles L. Todd and Robert Sonkin Migrant Worker Collection, 1940–1941.
Available at the Library of Congress Web site: http://memory.loc.gov/cgi-bin

THINK ABOUT THIS

Despite his misery, do you think this migrant worker has a sense of
humor?

"Dear Mrs. Roosevelt"— A Teenager Makes a Request

Eleanor Roosevelt received numerous requests for help from the
poor and unemployed. Many of the letters came from children
and teenage boys and girls whose parents were barely able to give
them food and clothes. Toys, bicycles, and sports equipment were

simply beyond the means of many families, but boys and girls of course still yearned for them. In the following letter, a teenage boy asks Mrs. Roosevelt for help.

42-06 159 Street
Flushing, New York
Mar. 22, 1934

"Please answer even if you can't do anything for me."

Dear Mrs. Roosevelt,

Please excuse the paper. I have never asked anybody for anything before and I feel kind of awkward writing this.

I am in the second term in Flushing High School and have managed to buy notebooks and pad so far. This being the spring term spring football is in session. This being my favorite sport I am trying out for the team. I man-aged to loan from a boy friend shoulder pad, helmit, and football pants but he didn't have any luck in securing a pair of football shoes. Practise started yesterday. I wore snickers [sneakers] and had my ankle cut by a fel-low with shoe's on. I came home last night and spoke to my par-ents about getting a pair of shoes.

Children were not spared the hardships of the Great Depression.

I'm sure they would like me to have these but my father, who works three days a week makes only $13.44 on the Long Island State Park Commission said we could not afford them.

I thought one of your sons may have an old pair of football shoes they do not use now. I wear size eight.

Please answer even if you can't do anything for me.

Thanking you in advance,
C. K.

—*From* Dear Mrs. Roosevelt: The Letters. *Available at the New Deal Network Web site: http://newdeal.feri.org/eleanor*

Mining for Coal at the Age of Twelve

Coal miners were among the poorest and most abused workers in America before and during the Depression. Working under the most dangerous conditions for meager wages, the miners were near slaves to the coal companies. They lived in company-built houses, were paid in company-issued money, and were forced to buy their food and supplies in company-owned stores where prices were high. Their situation worsened during the 1930s when coal companies cut back production and shortened work hours.

In this excerpt, miner Fred Harrison describes his experiences as a child laborer in the drift coal mines of northern Missouri during the 1930s. A drift mine goes into a hill at a downward slant. The roof, already low, gets lower as the mine burrows into the hill. Miners crawl on their stomachs to get at the coal, which they place in a low car and push along in front of them.

Coal mining is a dangerous and difficult job. Laws passed during the Great Depression finally helped keep children out of the mines, ensuring that no child under eighteen years of age could be employed in such a hazardous occupation.

"Many a boy begins in the mine when he's nine or ten."

I BEGAN IN THE DRIFT MINE when I was twelve. According to law, you must be sixteen before you start, but there's also a provision that a miner can take his son in to work with him. Many a boy begins in the mine when he's nine or ten. Of course, he can't do as much as a man, but he can pick up chunks [of coal] and

prop-caps
supports used to hold up the roof of a mine

put them in a car being loaded, and he can fetch prop-caps when his old man is putting in a narrow cutting or using the riddle.

One of my first jobs was to shake the riddle. The riddle is a coarse sieve through which the fine coal is sifted, the fine stuff falling to the ground to be shoveled separately into a car. This fine coal is sold later as "slack" at a lower price than the coarser lumps, which the man holding the sieve tosses into another car. The riddle

greenhorn
new worker

man usually sits cross-legged, and for the greenhorn it's an extra-tiring job having to sit there and feel the shock of each shovelful of coal thrown into it. . . .

The air [in the mine] is bad most of the time and it makes you sleepy and gives you a headache. . . .

There is a good deal of waste material after the coal is loaded. Soapstone falls from the roof, and there are sulphur streaks in the coal itself. The streak has to be picked out if it is too big, for the weigh boss gives you a dirty mark for every lump of soapstone or sulphur-filled coal you send to the top. When the dirty marks tally too much, you hear about it.

—From Ann Banks, First-Person America. *New York: Alfred A. Knopf, 1980.*

Berry Pickers Wanted

Joblessness forced many men and women to leave their homes and travel the nation in search of work. Country people moved to the cities in hope of getting jobs, and city people roamed around the countryside looking for the same. In the following selection, John Macnamara recalls his summer spent picking berries in New York State.

ABOUT THE FIRST OF JULY, after nine months of searching for a job in New York, I took to the road with two dollars in my pocket on the chance of getting summer work in the country. In the middle of July I reached Newburgh [a city on the Hudson River about one hundred miles north of New York City]. The National Reemployment Service [a New Deal program] in that town had nothing to offer me, but an advertisement in the local newspaper said that berry pickers were wanted at a place seven miles up the river. I arrived at dusk and the farmer said: "A cent and a half a quart. You feed yourself. Come up to the shack and I'll see if I can find a cot for you." . . .

This farm is planted entirely in fruit—apples, pears, and grapes. In the young orchards currant bushes are planted in the rows, raspberry bushes between the rows. Each picker has a "carrier"—a tray with a handle which holds eight quart boxes. . . .

At about eight o'clock [in the morning] the "families" began to arrive from Newburgh and the surrounding country—a father and mother and [several] children in a Ford car. They rapidly picked the best rows. . . .The children moved up and down the row with nimble fingers. The parents scolded or cajoled as the hot day wore on and the kids whined or sulked under the monotonous work. Their ages ranged from six to twelve or thirteen. A few days later I happened to be present when this family was cashing its ticket.

"I worked seven days . . . with a net profit of ninety-eight cents."

[Workers carried a ticket that the farmer punched when they turned in their berries and then exchanged the ticket for cash.] For one day's work of nearly ten hours the father collected for himself, his wife, and four children $2.44. . . .

I quit at five and went downtown to buy food. It is a two-mile walk to the village. . . . Bread and beans, a cigarette—and then add up the punches on the ticket. First day twenty-three quarts, thirty-four and a half cents.

I worked seven days and then took to the road again, with a net profit of ninety-eight cents.

—From "Berry Picker," in The Nation, September 12, 1934. Available at the New Deal Network Web site: http://newdeal.feri.org/nation/lna34302.htm

THINK ABOUT THIS

Do you think the author thought his trip to Newburgh was worth the effort?

Life on the Assembly Line

The 1930s were marked by episodes of violent labor unrest despite the National Industrial Recovery Act's protection of workers' right to organize and the setting of minimum wages and maximum hours. In the view of many workers, the act did not go far enough. A wave of strikes followed its passage. In 1934 there were 1,800 work stoppages involving more than 1.4 million workers. They included assembly-line workers, book and magazine editors, textile workers, and others. Playwright Clifford Odets even wrote a play about a strike called *Waiting for Lefty.*

American industrial workers, especially those in automobile assembly plants, were upset over wages, shutdowns, hiring practices, and working conditions. Above all, they demanded the right to bargain collectively with their employers, but employers

ORGANIZE?

WITH 1,250,000 WORKERS BACKING US

OF COURSE WE WILL ORGANIZE

During the 1930s organized labor struggled hard to make its voice heard. With support from the Roosevelt administration, the decade's labor movement would accomplish important changes in American industry.

refused to talk with the labor unions and instead formed company unions. Employment was based on membership in the company union. Workers' unions went on strike to pressure businesses into meeting their demands. In the following selection from a 1933 investigative report by Carl M. Mydans, the writer describes why the workers at a Ford Motor Car assembly plant went out on strike.

THE REAL OBJECT OF THE STRIKE at the Edgewater, New Jersey plant of the Ford Motor Car Company was, of course, a wage

Striking Ford workers take to the street. During the Great Depression, workers throughout the nation often went out on strike in an effort to improve their wages and working conditions.

increase. The workers seized the opportunity, however, to protest against a number of the conditions under which they had been working.

knack off
stop work

A breakdown on any part of the assembly line means that they all must knack off. The moment this happens, the time is recorded and the worker's pay stops. If the tie-up is for two hours, he must work two hours longer that night. In the meantime he is not permitted to leave his station.

"Ford pays his men on their time, not on his."

Frequently production reaches a point where it is necessary to shut down early in the day. Very often this breaking-point is at noon. But the men are never advised of this until after they have bought and eaten their lunch at the Ford restaurant. Then they are dismissed for the day, their pay covering only those hours which they have worked.

If a man is one minute late he is docked fifteen minutes. No provision is made for a worker to leave his post at any time for any reason while the "line" is moving.

The men are given a half-hour for lunch. They are paid twice a month—during their lunch hour. On pay days they must stand in line during this period eating their food. Those who are still in line when the 12:30 gong sounds must come back after work that night and stand in line again, or wait until the lunch hour of the following day. Ford pays his men on their time, not on his.

—*From "Why Ford Workers Strike," Carl M. Mydans, in*
The Nation, *October 25, 1933. Available at the New Deal Network*
Web site: http://newdeal.feri.org/nation/na33482.htm

THINK ABOUT THIS

1. What are some of the workers' grievances?

2. Why does the owner pay the workers on their lunch break?

Chapter 4

The Depression as Seen By . . .

THE DEPRESSION TOUCHED THE LIVES of all Americans. Workers in their prime felt a sense of personal defeat when they were thrown out of their jobs. Unemployed mothers and fathers tried desperately to keep their children housed, clothed, and fed. Men and women wore out their shoes walking the city streets searching for work. Those who were lucky to have jobs may have earned enough to get by but not enough to save. They also feared that any complaint might mean the loss of their job to someone hungrier or more desperate than they were. People were terrified of falling into debt because they were afraid they might never be able to get out.

Children especially felt the sting of hard times. Those who stayed in school often went there hungry and weak. Some boys and girls chose to stay home because they were embarrassed by their worn clothing. Many children dropped out of school to work in sweatshops, mills, mines, and other places that hired seasonal, part-time, or temporary workers. These child workers received a pittance of a wage, which they turned over to their parents.

During 1933, the worst year of the Depression, 25 percent of workers—
nearly 13 million Americans—were unemployed. Here a group of men wait
outside a state employment office in California, hoping to find jobs.

Ashamed of not being able to help out their parents, older children left home and school behind and wandered the countryside by foot or by rail.

Many of the voices you will hear in the following chapter are those of writers and artists—a famous photographer, a songwriter, a journalist, a budding playwright, men and women who honed their skills and earned their daily bread working for the Federal Writers' Project. This is how they saw the Great Depression.

A Fourteen-Year-Old Hobo

The Depression uprooted many Americans. They drifted from state to state looking for work or, giving up on the idea of finding

work, drifted because there was nothing else to do. In 1933, there were between one and two million people on the road. Adult men made up the majority of these vagrants or "hoboes." There were young hoboes, too. More than 200,000 young Americans were homeless in the early years of the Depression. Many were

At the height of the Depression, millions of hoboes roamed the country, catching illegal rides on freight trains.

school dropouts who lived by their wits on the streets, surviving on handouts, and even stealing. Others took to traveling around the countryside, hitching rides with strangers or riding freight trains.

Riding freight trains was especially dangerous. It was illegal and if caught by the railyard guards, the offender could be beaten, or jailed, or both. Towns and cities did not welcome hoboes. The police warned them to "keep moving." The following description of "riding the rails" was written by Eluard Luchell McDaniel. He was fourteen years old when the events described here took place.

IN THE WINTER OF 1931, three bums and myself began to see California by a I-O-U. About twenty-five cents among the four of us. Sleeping in the most comfortable box cars in the Southern Pacific Railroad yard. There were no hotels in the city of Los Angeles for the price we had to pay. . . .

At that time the hitch-hiking was not so good. People were afraid to trust strangers in their automobiles. The people that would give anyone a ride, did not want their car dirtyed up by bums like us. We done most of our traveling by train. In the railroad yard floaters were from all parts of America. The railroad Bulls were plentiful. They stayed busy trying to keep bums from riding the trains. Policemen were busy ordering floaters out of towns throughout California.

Some of the guys was from California, [but] most came from the North, South, and East. There was no trouble to find gangs from everywhere. Some floaters could tell you every railroad stop from the Atlantic to the Pacific. There were four in our group: Luchell McDaniel, B. Jay Hubert, Asti Butt Slim, and Mulligan Joe. . . .

I-O-U
abbreviation for "I owe you"

floaters
slang for "vagrants"

Bulls
slang for "guards"

The railroad Bull put us off the trains from Los Angeles. Walking taken place [they had to walk]. We seen a milepost. It showed six miles from Los Angeles city limit, on the road . . . and no stops. Not one had enough money to buy food for the group. We were saving the twenty-five cents for ferry fare into San Francisco. When we were three miles past San Bernardino, Asti spied some farmer's ranch. That ranch had peaches, grapes, and apricots. We made ourselves at home. We had our pockets full.

"Not much high talking and laughing. . . . The talk were food."

We rode the Fireball Special for three hours and twenty minutes. Another unhappy stop. Most of the fruit from the ranch had almost petered out. Not much high talking and laughing. No one cared about how large New York was, or how small the next town. The talk were food.

—From Eluard Luchell McDaniel, Bumming in California, *New York: The Viking Press, 1937, pp. 112–118. Copyright 1937 by the Guilds' Committee for Federal Writers' Publications, Inc. Available at the New Deal Network Web site: http://newdeal.feri.org/texts/614.htm*

THINK ABOUT THIS

Why do you think the vagrants were treated the way they were?

John and Jane Doe at the Employment Service

The Federal-State Employment Service came into existence in 1933 at the same time that government relief agencies were started. Many people thought the new organization would be only a temporary measure during a time of economic distress. But the agency became a permanent fixture. Its job is to help match workers with employers. The following article appeared in the *Fort Wayne Journal-Gazette* in 1937, advising people how to use the new service.

HOW DOES JOHN OR JANE DOE go about getting a job in Fort Wayne? One of his best bets will be to get in touch with the Indiana State Employment service if he or she is not already registered and included in the files of that far-reaching organization, an affiliate of the United States Employment Service. . . . It serves as a clearing house for labor, and when an employer makes a request for a specific type of man for a certain job, the employment office is concerned only with the man in its files who has the ability and can meet the requirements of that job.

"How does John or Jane Doe go about getting a job in Fort Wayne?"

"But, get this," Mr. Foster [manager of the Fort Wayne office] said, "we do not do the hiring of the men and women whom we call at the request of the employer. After a thorough check of our files we select the ones who appear most likely to meet the requirements and send them to the employer. He has the prerogative of accepting or rejecting them for the position."

The majority of clearance orders now are for skilled tradesmen, such as tool and die makers, first class machinists, and production machine operators, but requests have even been known to ask for a corporation lawyer to fill a $10,000 a year job.

A distinct shortage exists in the field of women workers, especially in the commercial class which includes trained secretaries, bookkeepers, sales women, etc. . . .

Here's a tip for applicants. It was found in digging for this story that the interviewers have an aversion for male applicants who are unshaven, and girls who snap their gum, wear brilliant nail polish, or who are heavily "mascared."

—From Robert D. Adams, "John Doe Gets His Job through the Indiana State Employment Service," in the Fort Wayne Journal-Gazette, October 3, 1937. Available at the New Deal Network Web site: http://newdeal.feri.org/ftwayne/fw004.httm

THINK ABOUT THIS

1. According to the article, what specific benefits did the service provide to job applicants? To employers?

2. Have "tips" for job applicants changed much since the time this was written?

Woody Guthrie's Dust Bowl Refugees

Many farmers were made homeless by one of the greatest natural disasters in the history of the world—a series of wind and dust storms of terrible proportions that struck the United States in the 1930s. The winds caused the most damage in the southern Great Plains, which came to be called the Dust Bowl. The states hardest hit were Colorado, Kansas, New Mexico, Oklahoma, and Texas, while bordering states also suffered.

Decades of overgrazing and poor farming methods—the wheat that the farmers grew did not adequately protect against soil erosion—had left the land vulnerable to wind and weather. These conditions were made worse by a long and terrible drought. It was

After drought forced them to give up their homes and property, farmers and their families watched as their possessions were sold at the auction block.

a prescription for disaster. The drought began in 1931 and lasted for seven years. In November 1933 one of the first major storms struck. Beginning in South Dakota, the great black dust storm blew long and hard. When the wind died down, the farmland that was once planted with wheat was covered by sand—mounds of it, in places. Farmhouses, barns, and machinery were coated with it. The dust storms continued into 1938. Unable to work the land, farmers and their families packed their belongings into their cars and trucks, abandoned their farms, and headed west to California for what they hoped would be a better life. They were the refugees from the Dust Bowl whom John Steinbeck immortalized in his novel *The Grapes of Wrath.*

A poster advertising a New Deal program to help victims of the Dust Bowl

YEARS OF DUST

RESETTLEMENT ADMINISTRATION
Rescues Victims
Restores Land to Proper Use

Woody Guthrie was a singer and songwriter, born in Oklahoma in 1912, who experienced the Dust Bowl firsthand. During his career, Guthrie wrote many songs about the lives of workers, farmers, and the poor. He died in 1967. The following lyrics are from Guthrie's "Dust Bowl Refugees."

I'm a dust bowl refugee,
Just a dust bowl refugee.
From that dust bowl to the peach bowl,
Now that peach fuzz is a-killin' me.

'Cross the mountains to the sea
Come the wife and kids with me.
It's a hot old dusty highway
For a dust bowl refugee.

Hard, it's always been that way,
Here today and on our way.
Down that mountain, 'cross the desert,
Just a dust bowl refugee.

We are ramblers so they say,
We are only here today.
Then we travel with the seasons,
We're the dust bowl refugees.

From the southland and the droughtland
Come the wife and kids with me.
And this old world is a hard world
For a dust bowl refugee.

Yes we ramble and we roam.
And the highway, that's our home.
It's a never-ending highway
For a dust bowl refugee.

Yes, we wander and we work
In your crops and in your fruit.
Like the whirlwinds on the desert,
That's the dust bowl refugees.

*"It's a hot old
dusty highway
For a dust bowl
refugee."*

—*From "Dust Bowl Refugees." Words and music by Woody Guthrie.*
© Copyright 1960 (renewed) and 1963 (renewed) Ludlow Music Inc., New York.
Available at http://www.geocities.com/Nashville/3448/refugee

THINK ABOUT THIS

1. Who is the narrator of this song?
2. What do you think Guthrie means by the "peach bowl"?
3. To what does Guthrie compare migrant workers?

Dorothea Lange, Photographer

The most famous photograph of the Great Depression *(opposite)* was taken in 1936 by Dorothea Lange. Shot in Nipomo, California, it portrays a migrant mother with three of her children in their tent. Lange never asked the woman's name, although she did learn her age: thirty-two. Dorothea Lange was born in 1895 and began her career as a studio photographer. In 1935 she went to work for the Farm Security Administration, a New Deal bureau. Lange gave her photographs of the homeless and of migrant farmworkers to newspapers for free. As they were printed, Americans gradually became aware of the plight of people they would never meet or talk with but who comprised the "forgotten" Americans. Lange died in 1965 at the age of seventy. Her photographs are among the most vivid documents of the Great Depression.

THINK ABOUT THIS

1. Why do you think this photo is the most famous image of the Depression?
2. Lange took several photos of this woman. You can find the others on the Library of Congress Web site.

Dorothea Lange's famous photograph of a Depression-era mother
and her children—a portrait of "forgotten" Americans

The Federal Writers

The Federal Writers' Project, part of the WPA, created one of the most lasting book series ever published with government funding. The Federal Writers wrote the American Guide Series in which each state in the country was covered in detail. Some of these guides can still be found in local libraries. The following selection is taken from *Minnesota: A Guide to the State* and describes the Twin Cities—Minneapolis and Saint Paul. The guide was written in 1938.

NUCLEUS OF THE NORTHWEST, in the hub of an area where 900,000 people live, the Twin Cities, Minneapolis and St. Paul, are at the head of navigation on the Mississippi River—1,596 miles from where it pours into the Gulf of Mexico—and near the geographical center of North America. Following the river, Minneapolis lies 15 miles upstream from St. Paul, but a crow flying from city hall to city hall would find them only 10 miles apart. Together, they form one metropolitan trade center, which ranks eighth in the United States.

"The visitor from the East will perhaps feel more at home in St. Paul; if from the West he is likely to prefer Minneapolis."

To a stranger they seem already to have merged. Connected by a common zone, each has grown up on both sides of the river, their residences intermingled; to the north only a surveyor's line divides them, farther south the mythical "center" of the river marks the boundary. But their citizens know that . . . each maintains . . . a personality differing sharply from that of its twin.

New York City Guide: one of the many titles in the American Guide Series produced by the Federal Writers' Project

Even the casual visitor (when he overcomes his bewilderment and determines into which city he has wandered), cannot fail to note certain obvious differences. The St. Paul skyline is all of a piece, Minneapolis sprawls; St. Paul is hilly, Minneapolis is level. . . . St. Paul's loop streets are narrow and concentrated, while in its twin city the center of activity extends many blocks along the broad shopping avenues. . . . St. Paul has already attained a degree of mellowness and seems to be clinging to its Victorian dignity, while in Minneapolis dignity is less prized than modern spruceness. The visitor from the East will perhaps feel more at home in St. Paul; if from the West he is likely to prefer Minneapolis.

—From Minnesota: A Guide to the State, *the Federal Writers' Project of the Works Progress Administration, Minnesota, November, 1938. Available at the New Deal Network Web site: http://newdeal.feri.org/guides/mn/title.htm*

THINK ABOUT THIS

1. Why do you think the federal government wanted a series of books about the states?

2. What were some of the differences between the Twin Cities in 1938?

Russell Baker, Journalist

In 1982, the Virginia-born journalist Russell Baker wrote a memoir about his experiences growing up during the 1930s. After his father's death in 1930, Russell's mother moved her small family first to Belleville, New Jersey, and then to Baltimore, Maryland. During this time, Russell lived with relatives and delivered newspapers while his mother sold magazine subscriptions door-to-door. Together, they experienced the struggle of staying alive. A selection from his book *Growing Up* follows.

The cover of Russell Baker's memoir, *Growing Up*

THE PAPER ROUTE EARNED ME three dollars a week, sometimes four and my mother, in addition to her commissions on magazine sales, also had her monthly check coming from Uncle Willie, but we'd been in Baltimore a year before I knew how desperate things were for her. One Saturday morning she told me she'd need Doris [Russell's sister] and me to go with her to pick up some food. I had a small wagon she'd bought me to make it easier to move the Sunday papers, and she said I'd better bring it along. The three of us set off eastward, passing the grocery stores we usually shopped at, and kept walking until we came to Fremont Avenue, a grim street of dilapidation and poverty. . . .

"This is where we go," she said when we reached the corner of

Fremont and Fayette Street. It looked like a grocery, with big plate-glass windows and people lugging out cardboard cartons and bulging bags, but it wasn't. I knew very well what it was.

"Are we going on relief?" I asked her.

"Don't ask questions about things you don't know anything about," she said. "Bring that wagon inside."

I did, and watched with a mixture of shame and greed while men filled it with food. None of it was food I liked. There were huge cans of grapefruit juice, big paper sacks of cornmeal, cellophane bags of rice and prunes. It was hard to believe all this was ours for no money at all, even though none of it was very appetizing. My wonder at this free bounty quickly changed to embarrassment as we headed home with it. Being on relief was a shameful thing. People who accepted the government's handouts were scorned by everyone I knew as idle no-accounts without enough self-respect to pay their own way in the world. I'd often heard my mother say the same thing of families in the neighborhood suspected of being on relief. These, I'd been taught to believe, were people beyond hope. Now we were as low as they were.

Pulling the wagon back toward Lombard Street, with Doris following behind to keep the edible proof of our disgrace from falling off, I knew my mother was far worse off than I'd suspected. She'd never have accepted such shame otherwise. I studied her as she walked along beside me, head high as always, not a bit bowed in disgrace, moving at her usual quick, hurry-up pace.

"Are we on relief now, Mom?"

If she'd given up on life, she didn't show it, but on the other hand she was unhappy about something. I dared to mention the dreaded words only once on that trip home.

"Are we on relief now, Mom?"

"Let me worry about that," she said.

—*From Russell Baker,* Growing Up, *New York: Congdon & Weed, 1982.*

Is being on relief still a source of shame today?

Students at DeWitt Clinton High

DeWitt Clinton High School in the Bronx, part of New York City, was an all-boys' school famed for its academic excellence. Graduates included writer James Baldwin, photographer Richard Avedon, and screenwriter Paddy Chayefsky. The school's literary magazine, *The Magpie,* contained short stories, poems, drawings, and photographs from the student body. One short story, "Collector's Job" by Henry J. Antupitsky, is included here. In it, the young writer imagines a day in the life of a man employed as a debt collector for a school.

THE BROWN DOOR OPENED UP its gaping jaws and yawned at him. He rang the bell and took out his slips.

"Collector, madam."

Thick lips and small eyes leered at him.

"No money. My husband is out of work for months. We . . ."

He interrupted her wearily.

"But we cannot support your child, madam. Our . . . situation demands that you pay or that your child leaves school."

She was going to cry. He saw the tears welling in her eyes. He hated people who wept. He himself had wept too much in the last few weeks before he got his job.

"You will get a call from the central office, madam. Good day."

He walked down the three flights of stairs. In the street, the hush of the night was disturbed rhythmically at even intervals by passing trains. The trolley cars and autos as they passed repeated in a weird metre:

"Out of a job. My husband is not working. I can't pay."

The big blotch of filthy water he passed seemed to be the woman's tears throwing themselves into his face. He closed his eyes trying to shut it all out of his mind. He looked at the slip in his hand. The next one was ten blocks up. . . . He was working only two hours. . . . That meant eighty cents. How would he exist? He was making only a dollar a day . . . about five dollars a week. He shook his head in despair and tramped wearily up the reeking street.

"No money. My husband is out of work for months."

He braced himself and rang the bell.

"Collector, madam."

And again there followed the usual procedure of talk . . . again that ill luck.

"My husband is out of work. We can't pay."

Again he told them of the school's sorely tried finances. He felt the words still ringing in his ears.

"Can't pay. Husband out of work."

Wearily, he walked on.

He searched the letterbox for the name. It was so dark; why couldn't they have a light there? There was a growing pain in his legs and a whirling sound in his head. . . . He peered intently into the dark, rang the first bell within his reach, and entered the hall.

As he climbed the four stories, he held on to the railing. The . . . odor of fried fish met his hungry nostrils and he began to be aware of a gnawing emptiness in his stomach. . . . He rang the bell.

"Collector, madam."

A small, eager face met his eyes.

"Come right in, please."

She led him into a dungeon reeking with poverty and need.

"Sit down, please."

He declined, afraid that if he sat down, he would never be able to get up.

"Have you change?"

He shook his head ruefully as she went out and he gazed longingly at the chair and the set table.

On her return, he gave her a receipt and left. Again he was ringing the bell. And again the black obscurity of the door opened up to him. . . .

"Collector, madam."

A pair of beady black eyes met his tired ones angrily.

"So . . . what do they want money for? The bills they send me. You tell them at the office that. . . ."

Her voice became dull and monotonous. . . . mixed and jumbled. Her face and lips were whirling around him in crazy circles. He closed his eyes for a moment . . . sighed, and sank to the ground. . . .

Dr. Cohen was speaking to his assistant, an intern interested in psychology.

"Exhaustion, hunger, and the continuous repetition of a certain phrase which kept hammering itself . . . on his brain. He needs rest and quiet."

The intern, puffed up with his knowledge . . . turned to Dr. Cohen.

"That has a technical term. It is called . . ."

Dr. Cohen motioned him to be quiet as the phone rang. It was his wife.

There was a collector there.

"Strange," said he, "we have one here, too."

"But he wants money."

"Money? Tell him we can't pay. I am out of work," and with this he hung up.

—From Henry J. Antupitsky, "Collector's Job," in The Magpie, June 1932, Vol. 33, No. 2, p. 5. Available at the New Deal Network Web site: http://newdeal.feri.org/magpie/docs

THINK ABOUT THIS

1. Why do you think the protagonist of this story took on the job of debt collector?

2. Does the ending come as a surprise?

Harold Ickes, on a Break with FDR

Harold Ickes was secretary of the interior during the presidency of Franklin Roosevelt. Born in Pennsylvania in 1874, Ickes left home at the age of sixteen and moved to Chicago. Upon graduating from the University of Chicago, Ickes worked as a reporter for various newspapers in the city, studied the law, and eventually became a lawyer. He became part of FDR's cabinet in 1933 and held his post until 1946. Harold Ickes kept a diary of the first thousand days of the Roosevelt administration and wrote the following description of the president at Warm Springs, Georgia.

President Roosevelt's personal car was fitted with special hand controls that allowed him to drive without using his legs.

FDR, who had polio, often visited this thermal spring and its treatment center, which he built to help other victims of the disease.

Wednesday, November 29, 1933

Saturday afternoon . . . I took the train for Atlanta, Georgia. . . . Colonel McIntyre . . . drove me over to Warm Springs, where I was the personal guest of the President. He has a small cottage . . . located on the edge of a well-wooded ravine just a little way out of Warm Springs. The President is always charming but he was delightful at Warm Springs. Everyone there loves him, and crowds hang outside the gate . . . just to see him and cheer him. . . . Some of the surrounding country is very lovely, and while I was there he took me driving on two or three occasions. He goes anywhere in his car [FDR's car was fitted with hand controls for the gas and brake], right into the woods, taking a real delight in making it difficult for the Secret Service car to follow him. I have never had contact with a man who was loved as he is. To the people of Warm Springs he is just a big jolly brother. They swarm all over him. . . . One woman whose legs were badly crippled with infantile paralysis was hoisted onto my side of the car and sat on the edge of it . . . while she led in the singing of two or three songs for the President.

"Everyone there loves him, and crowds hang outside the gate . . . just to see him and cheer him."

—*From* The Secret Diary of Harold L. Ickes, The First Thousand Days, 1933–1936. *New York: Simon & Schuster, 1953.*

THINK ABOUT THIS

1. What aspect of FDR's personality impressed Ickes?
2. Why do you think the people of Warm Springs were particularly fond of FDR?

The Social Security Board was established under Roosevelt's watch to provide pensions for retired workers over age sixty-five. Never before had the U.S. government taken this kind of responsibility for its citizens.

Chapter 5

Life Changes . . . and Goes On

THE EFFECTS OF THE GREAT DEPRESSION and the New Deal's response to it were felt in ways large and small across the United States. For the first time, the government took responsibility for providing every American with a security net. Workers gained access to old-age pensions, the guarantee of a minimum wage, and limits on how many hours they could be asked to work. The desperate poor were given relief payments. Farmers gained government assistance in improving agricultural methods and for dealing with crop surpluses. The nation's system of roads, bridges, and parks was improved with government funding and work programs. An entire region experienced economic development and modernization as a result of a massive government program of dam building and electrification.

As the New Deal passed into history, American attitudes about government's role—especially the federal government's role—in their lives changed. The idea that government had a responsibility to care for the neediest of its citizens—the "ill-clad, ill-housed, and ill-fed" referred to by FDR in his inaugural address of 1937—began to take hold. While many Americans prided themselves on their self-sufficiency and ability to survive tough times, many more came to believe that only the federal government could provide real help for certain basic problems. The following sources deal with the way life evolved for Americans during the Depression.

Economic Security for All: The Social Security Act

The idea of the federal government taking responsibility for the economic security and the well-being of its citizens took hold in the United States during the Great Depression. Some states had social security laws in 1929, the year of the stock market crash. But the federal government did not enact a system of national, compulsory

A poster explains how the Social Security program works.

social security until 1935, when Congress passed the Social Security Act.

The core of the Social Security program was the old-age pension. This was a benefit paid to people over the age of sixty-five, the amount received being based on their prior earnings. The money to pay for the pensions was accumulated from taxes taken out of employees' paychecks and employers' payrolls, with the tax rate increasing over the years. A reserve fund was set up for future generations. The Social Security Act also provided for federal grants to help states aid the disabled, needy children, the old, and the poor. Several sections of the act are included here.

SECTION 1 For the purpose of enabling each State to furnish financial assistance . . . to aged needy individuals, there is hereby authorized . . . the sum of $49,750,000 and there is hereby authorized to be appropriated for each fiscal year thereafter a sum sufficient to carry out the purposes of this title.

SECTION 201 There is hereby created an account in the Treasury of the United States to be known as the "Old-Age Reserve Account."

SECTION 202 Every qualified individual shall be entitled to receive . . . beginning on the date he attains the age of sixty-five . . . an old-age benefit.

> *"There is hereby created an account in the Treasury of the United States to be known as the 'Old-Age Reserve Account.'"*

SECTION 401 For the purpose of enabling each State to furnish financial assistance, as far as practicable under the conditions in such State, to needy dependent children, there is hereby authorized to be appropriated . . . the sum of $24,750,000 . . . to carry out the purpose of this title.

—*From* U.S. Statutes at Large, *Vol. XLIX, p. 620, in* Documents in American History. *Henry Steele Commager, editor. New York: Appleton-Century-Crofts, 1963.*

THINK ABOUT THIS

1. In addition to older Americans, who else is eligible to collect social security?

2. In your opinion, should social security be continued?

Let There Be Light

In the early 1930s, many rural areas of the United States—especially in the South—still had no electricity. By 1939 things had changed dramatically. The Rural Electrification Administration (REA), created in 1935, connected farmhouses to poles carrying electric lines and also helped set up rural electric cooperatives. Members bought their electricity from the cooperative. With access to electricity, farmers and others began to electrify their houses and introduce labor-saving devices. Here is how a farm woman in Kentucky describes how electrification has changed her life.

THE FIRST BENEFIT WE RECEIVED from the REA service was lights. . . . My little boy expressed my sentiments when he said, "Mother, I didn't realize how dark our house was until we got electric lights." We had been reading by an Aladdin lamp [oil or kerosene lamp] and thought it was good, but it didn't compare with our I.E.S. reading lamp [one approved by the Illuminating Engineering Society].

Recently, I read in the Rural Electrification News that the radio was the most popular appliance that had been bought. So, like the rest of the people, we changed our storage-battery radio into an electric radio. This was our next benefit.

Next we bought an electric refrigerator. . . . The next benefit we received from the current was our electric stove. We were so anxious for the current that we wired our house many months before the current was turned on, and we wired our kitchen for an electric range.

An Alabama woman prepares dinner on an electric stove. New Deal programs—the Rural Electrification Administration and the Tennessee Valley Authority— brought electricity to many areas for the first time.

Before the current was turned on, when anyone asked me what appliance I wanted most I always said that I wanted a vacuum cleaner. . . . I have an old-fashioned Brussells body carpet on my living-room floor, and when I swept it I raised as much dust as if I had been sweeping the dusty pike [road]. When I finished I was choking with the dust, the carpet was not clean, and I

"Mother, I didn't realize how dark our house was until we got electric lights."

was in a bad humor. Now with the vacuum cleaner, I can even dust the furniture before I clean the carpet, the carpet gets clean, and I stay in a good humor.

So you see I am thoroughly enjoying the many things that electricity had made possible, and I am enjoying life more.

—From Rose Dudley Scearce, Member, Shelby (Ky.) Rural Electric Cooperative, "What REA Service Means to Our Farm Home." Available at the New Deal Network Web site: http://newdeal.feri.org/tva

<u>THINK ABOUT THIS</u>

1. How did people read before electric lighting became available?

2. How would your life be different if you had no electricity?

Organizing the Workplace

Labor unions saw the economic crisis of the Great Depression as an opportunity to improve the lot of the American worker. Across the nation they struggled to organize workers into unions that would—through strikes and collective bargaining—force employers to improve wages and working conditions. Often companies would hire "scabs" to replace the workers who had gone out on strike, and sometimes violence would erupt between the two groups.

"Sit down! Sit down!"

As a result, workers, rather than leave their posts to stand in picket lines outside their companies, developed a new tactic: the sit-down strike. One of the most famous sit-down strikes of the Depression era took place in 1937, against General Motors in Flint, Michigan, by the United Auto Workers. In the following song a labor leader encourages workers to stand up to the bosses by "sitting down."

The famous sit-down strike of 1937 against General Motors in Flint, Michigan, forced management to negotiate with workers.

When they tie the can to a union man, sit down! Sit down!
When the speedup comes, just twiddle your thumbs,
Sit down! Sit down!
When the boss won't talk, don't take a walk.
Sit down! Sit down!

tying a can
focusing negative attention on a person

speedup
an increase in the speed of an assembly line

—*From R. L. Tyler,* Walter Reuther, *as quoted in* Freedom from Fear
by David M. Kennedy. New York: Oxford University Press, 1999.

1. According to the song, when should workers take action?
2. Why would assembly-line workers be angry if told to speed up?

The Old Job Disappears

Some workers during the Great Depression lost their jobs, and their self-respect, because of changes in technology, an ongoing process of the Industrial Revolution. When a new, highly mechanized steel mill went up in one town in Pennsylvania, 1,300 of the 1,500 steelworkers in the town were replaced by machines. In the following account we hear the voice of a highly skilled "old hand" lamenting the loss of his craft.

JUST BEFORE LEAVING the [new] mill I met Mike Michaels, an officer of the local union, sweeping up paper, bale tie ends, and dust in the shipping room. Mike came to America from Wales in 1904 at the age of fifteen. His father was one of the experienced Welsh hand-mill workers the company imported to run the now abandoned sheet mill when it was first built. Mike had worked there himself for over thirty years until it was closed last year. For twenty years he was a roller, an "aristocrat of labor," earning $12 to $15 a day. Now he was doing a laborer's job, at 63 cents an hour. Less than two hundred of the fifteen hundred displaced sheet mill workers in Steelville found jobs in the [new] strip mill. "What do you think of her?" Mike asked.

"It's impressive," a friend with me replied, "impressive—all that big automatic machinery running virtually without manpower. . . . " Mike leaned on his broom and with some bitterness said: "Impressive, huh! I'd call it oppressive, I would. Here I am pushing a broom, where I started over thirty years back. I'm not an old man yet. I've not turned fifty. But I'm too old to work on any of that impressive, I call it oppressive, machinery. They got a bunch of button pushers running this mill, young palookas, I call them, just kids."

Mike pointed to the endless ceiling with massive machinery under it. "Look at her!" he said. "You know what we call her?—'The Big Morgue.' The few of us old hand-mill men that got something to do here ain't so bad off as the thirteen hundred or more fellows that are out starving on relief or struggling on WPA. When we meet on the street and get to talkin we call this 'the big Morgue,' the place where all our jobs went dead."

"You know what we call her?—'The Big Morgue.'"

—*From Harold J. Ruttenberg, "The Big Morgue," in* Survey Graphic, *April 1939.*
Available at the New Deal Network Web site: http://newdeal.feri.org/texts/363.htm

THINK ABOUT THIS

1. What happened to the worker described in this article?

2. Why was he called an "aristocrat of labor"?

3. Can you think of jobs in other industries that have been lost to machines since the Great Depression?

September 1940: members of the Colson family, tobacco farmers in Suffield, Connecticut, gather around the dining table to pose for a photo. Despite the hardships of the Great Depression, many families managed to stay together.

Epilogue

Remembering the Great Depression

While it was true that many people went without food, housing, and jobs during the 1930s, some families managed to find enough work and raise enough food to keep their lives intact. In the following interview, conducted in 1997, a student named Becky Bailey speaks with Marvell Hunt, an ordinary woman who lived in Utah during the Great Depression. Marvell Hunt recalls how she and her husband raised nine children during those hard times.

Becky Bailey: This is Becky Bailey interviewing Marvell Hunt on her memories of the Great Depression. . . . Marvell, how old were you during the Great Depression?

Marvell Hunt: Well, I was about nineteen.

BB: When and where were you born?

MH: I was born on September 15, 1909.

BB: Tell me a little about your family and your circumstances.

MH: Well, Don and I were married quite young; he was 18 and I was 17. We were married in the year of 1927, and we went to the courthouse here in Richfield [Utah] to be married. Then we went to Sevier and we had a home there that we lived in for quite a few years off in the fields. . . . We lived there for a few years; then we moved again. It seemed we were always moving for the betterment of Don's work. He worked on all kinds of jobs to make a living for us.

BB: What kinds of jobs did he have?

MH: He had road jobs, he had building jobs, he had church jobs. . . . Then he worked for the timber [company] a lot getting posts and wood, helping the farmers on their farms. . . . He sorted potatoes for quite a while. He was a builder for houses; . . . he was a jack of all trades and the master of many. He just worked wherever he could get work . . . and we were thankful that he was able to 'cause times were hard. The wages were very, very small. We only got a dollar or two; that was quite a bit of money. . . . So we had to make our money count. . . . I had jobs of all kinds throughout my life and I took my family. I'd go teach classes and sit my kids down to the side of me through the lesson.

"We had to make our money count."

BB: What do you remember most about the Depression?

MH: I remember it was awful hard times, and it was hard to get a hold of enough to buy a sack of flour. . . . We made our own breads, cooked our vegetables, bottled our fruits, raised our gardens. We did most of our own cooking. . . . Did it all ourselves; we hardly ever bought anything. There was a lot of fun, but a lot of work.

BB: How many kids do you have?

MH: We had nine kids, six girls and three boys.

BB: What was the impact of living in the Great Depression and how did it affect you?

MH: We did pretty well during the Depression, but it was hard. . . . We did a lot of sewing for my family and Don's. My mother-in-law and my mother helped me a lot; . . . Everybody worked through it. . . . There was many, many things we did, we practically made our own sports around home; . . . We made a lot of our own fun and our families did. . . . We got along pretty well. The kids learned to share; with that many kids we had to teach that in our home.

BB: Did you know about other people around you that were worse off than you?

MH: Yes, and if we could, we helped. We would always lend a helping hand if we could see they really needed it and we had something they could use; we would always give it to them.

—From interview with Marvell Hunt conducted by Becky Bailey for the Sevier County [Utah] Oral History project, December 19, 1997. Available at the New Deal Network Web site: http://newdeal.feri.org/sevier/interviews/395i.htm

Time Line

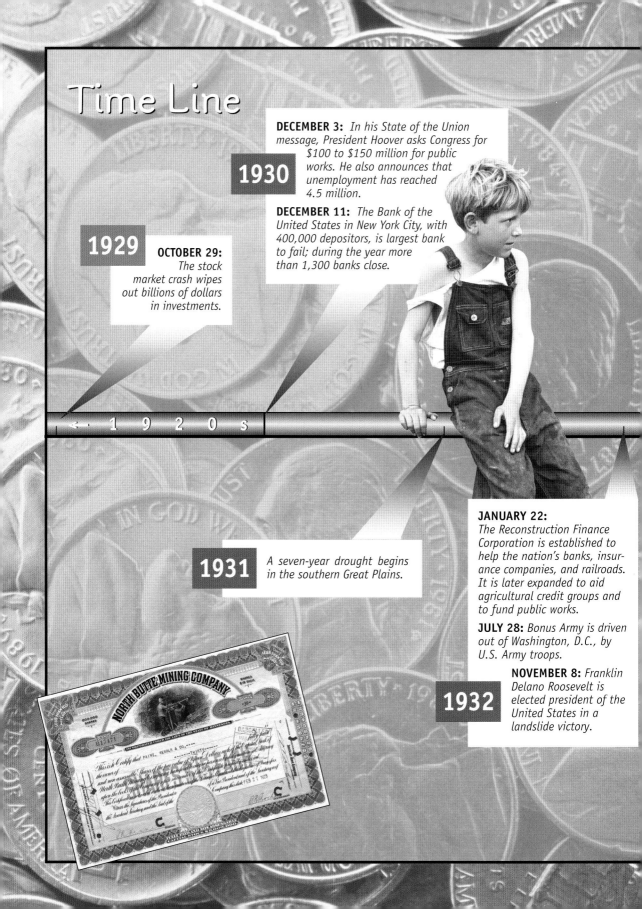

1930

DECEMBER 3: *In his State of the Union message, President Hoover asks Congress for $100 to $150 million for public works. He also announces that unemployment has reached 4.5 million.*

DECEMBER 11: *The Bank of the United States in New York City, with 400,000 depositors, is largest bank to fail; during the year more than 1,300 banks close.*

1929

OCTOBER 29: *The stock market crash wipes out billions of dollars in investments.*

← 1 9 2 0 s

1931 *A seven-year drought begins in the southern Great Plains.*

JANUARY 22: *The Reconstruction Finance Corporation is established to help the nation's banks, insurance companies, and railroads. It is later expanded to aid agricultural credit groups and to fund public works.*

JULY 28: *Bonus Army is driven out of Washington, D.C., by U.S. Army troops.*

NOVEMBER 8: *Franklin Delano Roosevelt is elected president of the United States in a landslide victory.*

1932

1933

FEBRUARY 14: *Governor of Michigan declares a one-day bank holiday. Other governors follow and begin to close banks in their states to keep panic-stricken depositors from withdrawing money.*

MARCH: *About 15 million Americans are unemployed, the worst month for joblessness in the nation's history.*

MARCH 6: *FDR declares a four-day national bank holiday as one of his first acts as president.*

← 1 9 3 0 s →

1935

APRIL 8: *The Works Progress Administration is established. It's later known as the Work Projects Administration.*

AUGUST 14: *The Social Security Act is passed.*

MAY 11: *The Rural Electrification Administration is established.*

JULY 5: *The National Labor Relations Board is established.*

1934

1934: *Dust storms spread over the southern plains and southwest, destroying millions of acres of farmland and forcing thousands of people to leave their homes.*

FEBRUARY 5: *Huey Long launches his "Share Our Wealth" program.*

JUNE 6: *The Securities and Exchange Commission is established to regulate stock exchanges and the trading of stocks.*

1937 — **JANUARY :** *Workers at the Flint, Michigan, plant of General Motors stage the first major sit-down strike in the United States.*

1938 — **JUNE 25:** *The Fair Labor Standards Act is passed by Congress. It establishes a national minimum wage of $0.25 per hour.*

← 1 9 3 0 s →

1939 — **SEPTEMBER 1:** *World War II breaks out in Europe when Germany invades Poland.*

SEPTEMBER 5: *President Roosevelt declares the United State neutral.*

APRIL 14: *The Grapes of Wrath by John Steinbeck is published.*

ORGANIZE

MANUFACTURING

WE DEMAND THE
NATIONAL TEXTILE ACT
KILL THE STRETCHOUT
HIGHER WAGES SHORTER HOURS
ORGANIZE
JOIN LOCAL
UNION
UNITED TEXTILE WORKERS OF AMERIC

MAY: *The Depression begins to ease as factories gear up to produce war supplies for nations at war with Germany.*

1940

JULY 19: *President Roosevelt signs an act of Congress providing for a navy of 200 ships.*

NOVEMBER 5: *President Roosevelt is reelected to a third term.*

1943

FEBRUARY 9: *President Roosevelt calls for a minimum work week of 48 hours for the duration of the war.*

1 9 4 0 s >

MARCH 11: *President Roosevelt signs Lend-Lease Act providing the loan of goods and munitions to democratic countries.*

1941

DECEMBER 7: *The Japanese attack Pearl Harbor.*

DECEMBER 8: *The United States declares war on Japan.*

DECEMBER 11: *Nazi Germany and Fascist Italy declare war on the United States. The United States then declares war on Germany and Italy.*

Glossary

assets items of ownership that can be converted into cash; also, the total resources of a person or business

bonds obligations, in written form, under which an individual corporation or government guarantees to pay a stated sum of money on or before a specific date

capital wealth, in the form of money or property, owned or used by an individual or business

depression a period during which employment, values of stock, and businesses decline or remain inactive

economy the way a nation's goods and services are produced, distributed, and used

infrastructure a nation's roads, ports, railways, bridges, dams, irrigation systems, etc. that enable businesses to move goods, farmers to raise and ship crops, and individuals to travel

relief money, food, and clothing given by the government to those in need during the Great Depression

shutdowns the closing of factories and businesses and the layoff of workers during a time of economic inactivity

social security a government program of guaranteed payments to the elderly, the unemployed, and the disabled made possible by a system of payroll deductions

speculation on the stock market, the trading in risky stocks in the hope of achieving great, quick gains

stock a share of ownership in a business or corporation

strike a work stoppage carried out by employees against an employer with the aim of forcing the employer to pay higher wages, improve working conditions, or shorten work hours

underconsumption an economic condition in which consumers, because of lack of money or confidence, buy less than what is readily available from a business, thus causing the business to fail

welfare government help given to those in need until they are able to take care of themselves

To Find Out More

BOOKS FOR OLDER READERS

Badger, Anthony J. *The New Deal: The Depression Years, 1933–1940.* New York: Farrar, Straus & Giroux, 1989.

Congdon, Don. *The Thirties: A Time to Remember.* New York: Simon & Schuster, 1962.

Frisch, Morton J., and Martin Diamond, editors. *The Thirties.* DeKalb, IL: Northern Illinois University Press, 1968.

Garraty, John A. *The Great Depression.* San Diego, CA: Harcourt Brace Jovanovich, 1986.

McElvaine, Robert S. *The Great Depression: America, 1929–1941.* New York: Three Rivers Press, 1984.

Phillips, Cabell B. H. *From the Crash to the Blitz, 1929–1939.* New York: Fordham University Press, 2000.

Thomas, Gordon, and Max Morgan-Witts. *The Day the Bubble Burst.* Garden City, NY: Doubleday, 1979.

Wecter, Dixon. *The Age of the Great Depression, 1929–1941.* New York: Macmillan, 1948.

BOOKS FOR YOUNG READERS

Nonfiction

Farrell, Jacqueline. *The Great Depression.* San Diego, CA: Lucent Books, 1996.

Fremon, David K. *The Great Depression in American History.* Berkeley Heights, NJ: Enslow Publishers, 1997.

Meltzer, Milton. *Brother, Can You Spare a Dime?: The Great Depression, 1929–1933* New York: Facts on File, 1991.

Stein, R. Conrad. *The Great Depression.* Chicago: Children's Press, 1993.

Fiction

Curtis, Christopher Paul. *Bud, Not Buddy.* New York: Delacorte Press, 1999.

Fenton, Edward. *Duffy's Rocks.* Pittsburg, PA: Golden Triangle Books, University of Pittsburgh Press, 1999.

Hesse, Karen. *Out of the Dust.* New York: Scholastic Press, 1997.

WEB SITES

The Web sites listed here were in existence in 2003–2004 when this book was being written. Their names or locations may have changed since then.

In general, when using the Internet to do research on a history topic, you should use caution. You will find numerous Web sites that are very attractive to look at and appear to be professional in format. Proceed with caution, however. Many, even the best ones, contain errors. Some Web sites even insert disclaimers or warnings about mistakes that may have made their way into the site. In the case of primary sources, the builders of the Web site often transcribe previously published material, good or bad, accurate or inaccurate. Therefore, you have to judge the content of *all* Web sites. This requires a critical eye.

A good rule for using the Internet as a resource is always to compare what you find in Web sites to several other sources such as librarian- or teacher-recommended reference works and major works of scholarship. By doing this, you will discover the myriad versions of history that exist.

http://memory.loc.gov/ammem/fsowhome.html
Photographs of the Great Depression.

http://newdeal.feri.org
A guide to the Great Depression and the New Deal.

http://www.fdrlibrary.marist.edu
The FDR Presidential Library and Museum.

www.fordham.edu/halsall/mod/modsbook41.html
Internet Modern History Sourcebook.

http://american history.about.com/cs
An overview of the Depression and the New Deal.

http://lcweb2.loc.gov

> Primary source materials, including WPA life histories, from the Library of Congress

http://www.pbs.org/wgbh/amex/dustbowl

> *The American Experience: Surviving the Dust Bowl.*

VIDEOS

Bound for Glory. Biography of folk singer and composer Woody Guthrie.

The Grapes of Wrath. Classic 1940 film based on John Steinbeck's novel of Okies' trek from the Dust Bowl to California.

The Journey of Natty Gann. Story of a young girl who travels across the country during the Depression to be with her father.

King of the Hill. 1993 film based on a memoir by A. E. Hotchner of a twelve-year-old boy growing up in St. Louis during the Depression.

Paper Moon. Story of a Depression-era con man who teams up with an unusually clever young girl.

Places in the Heart. A Texas widow struggles to keep her cotton farm during the Depression.

Sounder. The story of a black sharecropper family during the Great Depression.

Sullivan's Travels. Classic 1941 story of a Hollywood director who takes to the road to discover what it means to be poor.

Index

Page numbers for illustrations are in boldface

ABOUT THE AUTHOR

Adriane Ruggiero writes frequently about history, both ancient and modern, and international affairs. Her most recent publications include *The Baltic Countries: Estonia, Latvia, and Lithuania,* published by Silver Burdett Press; *The Byzantine Empire: A Cultural Legacy,* published by Golden Owl Press; and *The Crusades,* also published by Golden Owl Press. Ms. Ruggiero is also a frequent contributor to reference works such as *The Dictionary of the Middle Ages, The Encyclopedia of Ancient Greece and Rome,* and *Magill's Encyclopedia of Military History.* She resides in Teaneck, New Jersey.